Manfred Bojes

Grundwissen englische Grammatik

5./6. Klasse

W0221011

PERSEN

Gedruckt auf umweltbewusst gefertigtem, chlorfrei gebleichtem und alterungsbeständigem Papier.

1. Auflage 2012
© Persen Verlag, Buxtehude

3. Auflage 2015
© Persen Verlag, Hamburg
AAP Lehrerfachverlage GmbH
Alle Rechte vorbehalten.

Das Werk als Ganzes sowie in seinen Teilen unterliegt dem deutschen Urheberrecht. Der Erwerber des Werkes ist berechtigt, das Werk als Ganzes oder in seinen Teilen für den eigenen Gebrauch und den Einsatz im Unterricht zu nutzen. Die Nutzung ist nur für den genannten Zweck gestattet, nicht jedoch für einen weiteren kommerziellen Gebrauch, für die Weiterleitung an Dritte oder für die Veröffentlichung im Internet oder in Intranets. Eine über den genannten Zweck hinausgehende Nutzung bedarf in jedem Fall der vorherigen schriftlichen Zustimmung des Verlages.

Sind Internetadressen in diesem Werk angegeben, wurden diese vom Verlag sorgfältig geprüft. Da wir auf die externen Seiten weder inhaltliche noch gestalterische Einflussmöglichkeiten haben, können wir nicht garantieren, dass die Inhalte zu einem späteren Zeitpunkt noch dieselben sind wie zum Zeitpunkt der Drucklegung. Der Persen Verlag übernimmt deshalb keine Gewähr für die Aktualität und den Inhalt dieser Internetseiten oder solcher, die mit ihnen verlinkt sind, und schließt jegliche Haftung aus.

Grafik: Bert Breitenbach
Satz: Satzpunkt Ursula Ewert GmbH

ISBN: 978-3-403-23134-9

www.persen.de

Inhaltsverzeichnis

Vorwort

Das vorliegende Buch hat sich vor allem zum Ziel gesetzt, **Lehrkräfte** im Sekundarbereich I – vornehmlich der Jahrgänge 5 und 6 – in zweierlei Hinsicht **zu entlasten:**

1. Bei der Vermittlung grammatischer Inhalte

Immer wieder stehen Lehrerinnen und Lehrer vor der schwierigen Aufgabe, die Regel- und Ausnahmefälle neuer Strukturen in stark heterogen zusammengesetzten Lerngruppen vermitteln zu müssen. Hier können die Grammatikanhänge der Lehrwerke trotz aller Fortschritte leider nur eine recht eingeschränkte Hilfestellung bieten. Dies gilt in besonderem Maße für die Jahrgangsstufen 5 und 6, die häufig von Schülerinnen und Schülern besucht werden, die ursprünglich eine Schullaufbahnempfehlung für eine andere Schulform erhalten haben.

Die mangelhafte Einsatzfähigkeit der Grammatikanhänge liegt zum einen an dem Zwang für die Verlage, den Genehmigungsbehörden und dem kritischen Blick der Mitbewerber linguistisch unangreifbare Korrektheit anzubieten. Zum anderen soll den Richtlinien/Curricula/Lehrplänen möglichst vieler oder gar aller Bundesländer entsprochen werden, was zu einem Streben nach möglichst umfassender Darstellung jedes grammatischen Pensums im Grammatikanhang führt.

Beides hat zur Folge, dass die Erklärungen im **Grammatikanhang der Lehrbücher oft nicht zu den individuellen Erfordernissen der einzelnen Lerngruppen passen.**

An dieser Stelle setzt das vorliegende Konzept an, in dem grammatische **Regeln so formuliert sind, dass sie als „Gebrauchsanweisungen“** von möglichst allen Schülern **verstanden werden**. Dadurch muss die Lehrkraft keine wertvolle Vorbereitungs- und Unterrichtszeit darauf verwenden, die „Erklärung zu erklären“, d. h. grammatische Termini zu erläutern, gestelzte Formulierungen zu vereinfachen oder zu lange, geschachtelte Sätze für die Lernenden zu „übersetzen“.

Der Verfasser hat die Auswahl und Anordnung der grammatischen Inhalte nach einer Synopse der Richtlinien aller Bundesländer getroffen, um eine möglichst hohe Kongruenz für alle „Anwender“ in ganz Deutschland zu erzielen.

2. Bei der Erstellung und dem methodisch angemessenen Einsatz von Übungen

Im Sekundarbereich I müssen Lehrkräfte häufig erfahren, dass es **zu wenig Übungsmaterial** für grammatische Themen gibt. Das Reservoir des Übungsapparates im Zusammenhang mit dem Lehrbuch ist bald erschöpft. Die Lerngruppe wirkt jedoch noch erkennbar unsicher im Anwenden des neuen Sprachmaterials, sodass Lehrerinnen und Lehrer sich – meistens unter Zeitdruck – regelmäßig der Mühe unterziehen, selbstständig Übungen zu entwickeln, die in Umfang und Leistungsanforderung der einzelnen Klasse entsprechen. Aufgrund der Zeitnot bleibt kaum die Möglichkeit, solche Übungen auch noch situativ einzubetten.

© Persen Verlag

Hier setzt das Konzept der vorliegenden Übungen an:

1. Es gibt **zwei Schwierigkeitsstufen**. Die Aufgaben mit höherem Schwierigkeitsgrad sind mit * gekennzeichnet. Sie sollten nur in Lerngruppen mit gutem Realschulniveau und besser oder zur inneren Differenzierung eingesetzt werden. Die anderen Aufgaben sind zum „Einschleifen" der Strukturen für fast alle Lerngruppen verwendbar. Sie können daher auch sehr gut im Förder- und privaten Einzelunterricht und als Hausaufgabe eingesetzt werden, weil sie
   a) **selbsterklärend** sind und
   b) den Schülerinnen und Schülern durch den Einsatz **geläufiger Übungstypen** keine weiteren gedanklichen Operationen zur Lösung der Aufgaben abverlangen. Diese würden sich bei der Konzentration auf das Sprachmaterial störend auswirken.

2. Die Übungen spielen in **situativen Zusammenhängen**. Dieses Merkmal vermittelt den Schülerinnen und Schülern das Gefühl, dass Grammatik kein Selbstzweck ist, sondern eine kommunikative Funktion erfüllt. Darüber hinaus stellt diese Konzeption der Aufgaben erneut sicher, dass der Lerner sich nicht gedanklich bei jedem weiteren Satz innerhalb der Übung auf eine neue Situation einstellen muss. So entfällt eine der gedanklichen Operationen, die nichts mit der eigentlich im Mittelpunkt stehenden sprachlichen Leistung zu tun haben.

3. Innerhalb eines grammatischen Pensums zieht sich in der Regel ebenfalls ein **situativer roter Faden durch alle Aufgaben**, sodass sie auch als Einheit eingesetzt werden können. Jede Übung bleibt selbstverständlich trotzdem als solche einzeln verständlich und einsetzbar.

Viel Erfolg bei der Umsetzung in die Unterrichtspraxis wünscht Ihnen und Ihren Kolleginnen und Kollegen

Manfred Bojes

© Persen Verlag

1. Die Personalpronomen (persönliche Fürwörter)

Genau wie im Deutschen gibt es auch in der englischen Sprache Wörter, die **für** Personen, Tiere oder Gegenstände stehen. Aus diesem Grunde heißen sie auch persönliche **Für**wörter oder Personalpronomen.

a) In der Einzahl gibt es die Personalpronomen:

I = ich   you = du   he = er   she = sie   it = es

He steht für eine männliche Person, *she* für eine weibliche Person.

Ein Tier kannst du auch mit *he* oder *she* benennen, wenn du den Namen des Tieres kennst.

Für Tiere, deren Namen du nicht kennst, und für alle Sachen verwendest du einfach *it.*

Da das Englische die Anrede mit „Sie" nicht kennt, kann *you* daher auch „Sie" bedeuten.

Das Wort *I* schreibt man immer groß.

Beispiele:

Hi, **I** am Holly.	Hi, **ich** bin Holly.
Are **you** from Germany? Are **you** the new teacher?	Kommst **du** aus Deutschland? Sind **Sie** der neue Lehrer?
Look, Timmy. **He** is my brother.	Sieh mal, Timmy. **Er** ist mein Bruder.
Here is Lilly Cool. **She** is my mother. And this is Pussy. **She** is my cat.	Dies hier ist Lilly Cool. **Sie** ist meine Mutter. Und das ist Pussy. **Sie** ist meine Katze.
Here is my bike. **It** is new.	Dies hier ist mein Rad. **Es** ist neu.

b) In der Mehrzahl gibt es die Personalpronomen:

we = wir   you = ihr   they = sie

Wie du siehst, kommt das Wort *you* zweimal als Pronomen vor: es kann „du" oder „ihr" bedeuten.
Wie in der Einzahl kann *you* auch in der Mehrzahl in der Anrede für „Sie" stehen.

They kannst du für Personen, Sachen und Tiere verwenden.

Manfred Bojes: Grundwissen englische Grammatik – 5./6. Klasse
© Persen Verlag

Beispiele:

We are the Cool family.	**Wir** sind die Familie Cool.
Are **you** fine, Maxi and Molly? Are **you** the new teachers?	Geht es **euch** gut, Maxi und Molly? Sind **Sie** die neuen Lehrer?
Here are Maxi and Molly. **They** are my uncle and my aunt.	Dies sind Maxi und Molly. **Sie** sind mein Onkel und meine Tante.
Look at the two cars, **they** are new.	Guck mal, die zwei Autos, **sie** sind neu.
Ben has three cats, **they** are black and white.	Ben hat drei Katzen, **sie** sind schwarz und weiβ.

The Cool Family from Manchester

The Cool family tree

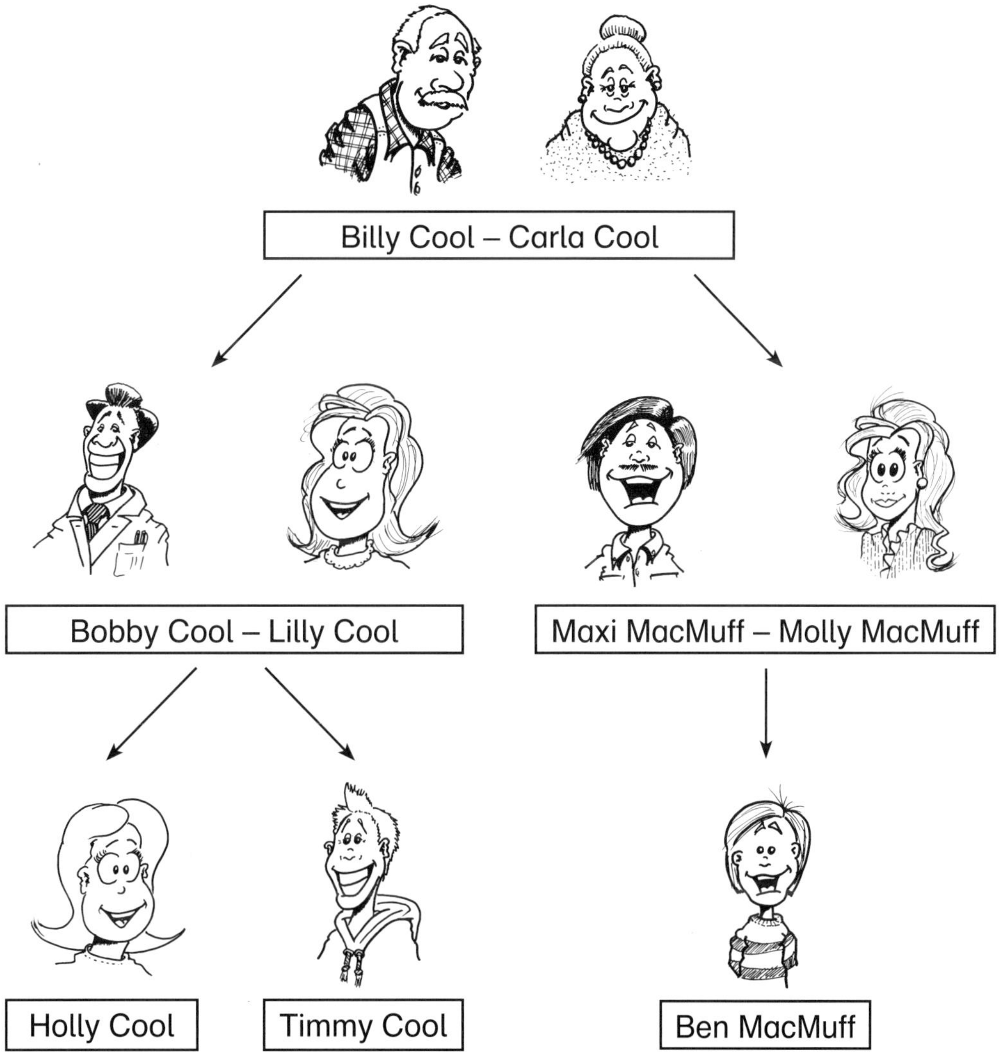

© Persen Verlag

Exercise 1	Cool pictures

Put in: *I – you – he – he – it – we – you – they*

1. Here is Timmy Cool.  __________ is Holly's brother.

2. Here is Bobby Cool.  __________ is Molly's brother.

3. Here is Billy's and Carla's house.  __________ is old.

4. Here are Holly and Ben.  __________ are cousins.

5. Lilly Cool:  "__________ am Holly's and Timmy's mother."

6. Billy and Carla:  "__________ are from Manchester."

7. Ben:  "__________ are my cousins, Holly and Timmy."

8. Holly:  "__________ are my uncle, Maxi."

Manfred Bojes: Grundwissen englische Grammatik – 5./6. Klasse
© Persen Verlag

Exercise 2	The Cools and the MacMuffs

Put in: *I – they (2×) – you (2×) – it – she (4×) – he – we (4×)*

Carla and Billy: "__________ are Carla and Billy, __________ are Bobby's parents."

Timmy: "__________ am Timmy. And here is Holly, __________ is my sister."

"Hi, Ben, are __________ Holly's sister?" – "No, __________ are cousins."

"Maxi and Molly, are __________ Timmy's parents?"

"No, __________ are Timmy's uncle and aunt. Look, here are Bobby and

Lilly. __________ are Timmy's parents."

"Is Carla Molly's mother?" – "Yes, __________ is Molly's mother."

"Is Ben Holly's cousin?" – "Yes, __________ is Holly's cousin."

"Is Pussy your cat, Holly?" – "Yes, __________ is my cat."

"Is that your black and white cat, Timmy?" – "No,

__________ is Ben's cat. __________ has three cats.__________ are all black and white."

© Persen Verlag

2. Das Verb *to be* I (Langformen)

To be ist die englische Entsprechung des deutschen Verbs „sein".
Du verwendest *to be*, wenn du etwas über den Zustand von Personen oder Gegenständen sagen möchtest. Genau wie im Deutschen ändert sich die Verbform, je nachdem, welche Person gerade gemeint ist:

I am	ich bin
you are	du bist (oder in der Anrede, wenn man eine Person siezt: „**S**ie sind …")
he is	er ist
she is	sie ist
it is	es ist
we are	wir sind
you are	ihr seid (oder in der Anrede, wenn man eine Gruppe von Personen siezt: „**S**ie sind …")
they are	sie sind

Diese Formen nennt man „Langformen". Du siehst sie vor allem in geschriebenen Texten. Deshalb benutze sie, wenn du selber auch einen Text schreibst.
Es ist aber nicht falsch, die Langformen auch beim Sprechen zu verwenden!

Beispiele:

I am from Manchester.
You are from Germany.
She is nice.
We are new here.
They are cousins.

Exercise 1	Holly's community entry

Cross out the wrong forms.

My name **is/are** Holly Cool. I **am/are** from Manchester. I **is/am** at St. Peter's School. Our school **are/is** not big, and the teachers **are/is** OK. My new friend **is/am** Barney. He **are/is** very nice! Pat and Lisa **are/is** my friends, too. They **am/are** from Goole Street. It **is/are** near here. Our hobby **are/is** Britpop music. My mother **am/is** a Britpop music fan, too!

Manfred Bojes: Grundwissen englische Grammatik – 5./6. Klasse
© Persen Verlag

Exercise 2	Timmy's birthday party

Put in the right forms of "to be".

It __________ Timmy's birthday party today. He __________ eleven. The Cools __________ at the party. His cousin __________ there, too. His name __________ Ben. He __________ thirteen. Carla Cool __________ not at the party. She __________ ill. What __________ that under the table? __________ there four cats? Yes, they __________ Holly's and Ben's cats.

Exercise 3	My community entry

Write a short entry about yourself for an internet community.

____

____

____

____

____

© Persen Verlag

3. Das Verb *to be* II (Kurzformen)

Beim Sprechen werden im Englischen oft ganze Silben verschluckt. Ähnliches geschieht beim Gebrauch der Formen von *to be*. Deswegen gibt es für alle Langformen von *to be* auch Kurzformen:

Langform	Kurzform	
I am	I'm	ich bin
you are	you're	du bist
he is	he's	er ist
she is	she's	sie ist
it is	it's	es ist
we are	we're	wir sind
you are	you're	ihr seid/Sie sind (beim Siezen)
they are	they're	sie sind

Du siehst: Überall da, wo ein Buchstabe weggefallen ist, steht jetzt ein Apostroph.

Die Kurzformen kannst du außer beim Sprechen auch benutzen, wenn du etwas Gesprochenes aufschreibst oder wenn du an Freunde oder gute Bekannte schreibst.

Beispiele:

Ben: "Hi, I'm Ben."
Timmy: "You're my cousin."
Ben and Timmy: "We're from Manchester."
Timmy: "Here's Holly. She's twelve."
Ben: "Look, Carla and Billy. They're our grandparents."
Holly: "St. Peter's is my school. It's not big."

Exercise 1	Can you find the short forms?

1. He ____ very cool.
2. She ____ Holly.
3. I ____ from Manchester.
4. It ____ OK.
5. You ____ my friend.
6. They ____ my cats.

Manfred Bojes: Grundwissen englische Grammatik – 5./6. Klasse
© Persen Verlag

Exercise 2	Can you find the long forms?

1. She's twelve. ______________________
2. We're at St. Peter's School. ______________________
3. You're at St. Peter's, too. ______________________
4. It's a small school. ______________________
5. He's my friend. ______________________
6. I'm in your class. ______________________
7. They're friends. ______________________

Exercise 3	At St. Peter's School

Put in: *I'm – you're – he's – she's – it's – we're – they're*

1. "Is Betty at your school, Timmy?" – "Yes, __________ new in my class."
2. "Where are Holly and Ben?" – "__________ in the playground."
3. "Is Ben from London?" – "No, __________ from Manchester."
4. "Are you twelve, Timmy?" – "No, __________ eleven."
5. "Are you and Ben cousins?" – "Yes, __________ cousins."
6. "Am I late, Mrs White?" – "Yes, Timmy, __________ late."
7. "What is that on the board?" – "__________ a picture of you, Mrs White."

© Persen Verlag

Exercise 4	**Twitter and mail from Betty**

Put in the short forms: *I'm – you're – he's – she's – it's – we're – they're*

a) Here is Betty's twitter to her friend from her old school in Cardiff.

Hi Gwen,

I hope __________ OK, Gwen. Here in Manchester __________ very nice. __________ at St. Peter's School. My new friends are Holly and Timmy. __________ great. __________ in one sports group. Ben MacMuff is a new friend, too. __________ Holly's and Timmy's cousin. My teacher is Mrs White. __________ not so nice.

b) Betty writes this as an email to her old teacher in Cardiff, too.

Use the long forms, please.

Hello Mr Dilwyn,

I hope __________ OK, Mr Dilwyn. Here ____________________________________

____

____

____

____

____ not so nice.

Manfred Bojes: Grundwissen englische Grammatik – 5./6. Klasse
© Persen Verlag

4. Das Verb *to be* III (Verneinung)

Wenn du *to be* verneinen möchtest, fügst du nach der Form von *to be*, die du gerade verwendet hast (*am, is* oder *are*), einfach nur *not* bzw. *-n't* ein.

Beispiele:

Langform:	Kurzform:
I am not from London.	I'm not from London.
You are not late, Timmy.	You aren't late, Timmy.
He is not twelve.	He isn't twelve.
She is not eleven.	She isn't eleven.
It is not a big school.	It isn't a big school.
We are not from Cardiff.	We aren't from Cardiff.
You are not new here, Holly and Timmy.	You aren't new here, Holly and Timmy.
They are not my cats.	They aren't my cats.

Nur ganz selten begegnest du auch diesen Kurzformen:
you're not – he's not – she's not – it's not – we're not – you're not – they're not

Von *I am not* gibt es nur die eine Kurzform: *I'm not*!

Exercise 1	It's all wrong!

Complete the sentences with the correct forms of "to be" and the correct personal pronouns. Use the short forms, please.

1. St. Peter's School __________ big. __________ small.
2. Mr Dilwyn __________ in Manchester. __________ in Cardiff.
3. Mrs White __________ in Cardiff. __________ in Manchester.
4. Maxi and Molly __________ Timmy's parents. __________ Ben's parents.
5. Ben and Timmy __________ girls. __________ boys.
6. Holly __________ eleven. __________ twelve.
7. Holly and Ben __________ sister and brother. __________ cousins.
8. Betty __________ Holly's sister. __________ Holly's friend.
9. The three cats __________ Lilly's cats. __________ Ben's cats.
10. Pat and Lisa __________ from Old Street. __________ from Goole Street.

© Persen Verlag

Exercise 2	Hide-and-seek at the birthday party

Where are they? Complete the sentences.

a) Use the short forms:

he's – he isn't | she's – she isn't | it's – it isn't

they're – they aren't | you're – you aren't

Example: Holly? She isn't on the table, she's under the table.

1. Timmy? __________ behind the cupboard, __________ behind the door.
2. Where is Barney? __________ behind the door, __________ under the table.
3. Where are Bobby and Lilly? __________ under the table, __________ in the cupboard.
4. Betty? __________ in the cupboard, __________ under a chair.
5. The cats? __________ under the chair, __________ in the window.

b) Now use the long forms, please.

Example: Holly? She is not on the table, she is under the table.

1. Timmy? ______________ behind the cupboard, ______________ behind the door.
2. Where is Barney? ______________ behind the door, ______________ under the table.
3. Where are Bobby and Lilly? ______________ under the table, ______________ in the cupboard.
4. Betty? ______________ in the cupboard, ______________ under a chair.
5. The cats? ______________ under the chair, ______________ in the window.

Manfred Bojes: Grundwissen englische Grammatik – 5./6. Klasse
© Persen Verlag

5. Das Verb *to be* IV (Fragen und Kurzantworten)

Wenn du Fragen stellst, in denen Formen von *to be* vorkommen, bildest du die Fragen genauso wie im Deutschen. Das heißt, im Deutschen beginnt die Frage mit einer Form von „sein“, im Englischen kommt eine Form von *to be* an den Anfang.

Beispiele:

Am I late, Mrs White?	**Bin** ich zu spät, Mrs White?
Are you in class 7?	**Bist** du in Klasse 7?
Is he from Cardiff?	**Ist** er aus Cardiff?
Is she a friend?	**Ist** sie eine Freundin?
Is it nice at St. Peter's?	**Ist** es nett auf der St.-Peter-Schule?
Are we in Mrs White's new class?	**Sind** wir in Mrs Whites neuer Klasse?
Are you cousins?	**Seid** ihr Cousins?
Are they brother and sister?	**Sind** sie Geschwister?

Du musst bei der Fragebildung also gar nichts Neues lernen.

Nur die einzelnen Formen von *to be* solltest du ab jetzt perfekt beherrschen. Du wirst sie immer wieder brauchen!

Willst du auf eine Frage mit „ja“ oder „nein“ antworten, könnte es ein wenig unhöflich wirken, wenn du nur *yes* oder *no* sagst. Im Englischen antwortet man nämlich fast immer mit einem kurzen Satz, den man auch „Kurzantwort“ nennt.

Beispiele:

	Kurzantworten:	
Am I late, Mrs White?	Yes, **you are**.	No, **you aren't**.
Are you in Class 7?	Yes, **I am**.	No, **I'm not**.
Is he from Cardiff?	Yes, **he is**.	No, **he isn't**.
Is she a friend?	Yes, **she is**.	No, **she isn't**.
Is it nice at St. Peter's?	Yes, **it is**.	No, **it isn't**.
Are we in Mrs White's new class?	Yes, **you are**.	No, **you aren't**.
Are you cousins?	Yes, **we are**.	No, **we aren't**.
Are they brother and sister?	Yes, **they are**.	No, **they aren't**.

© Persen Verlag

Exercise 1	**Can you remember?**

Make short answers.

1. Is Betty from London?

    ______________________________.

2. Is Betty's hobby Britpop music?

    ______________________________.

3. Betty: "Am I in your sports group, Timmy?"

    ______________________________.

4. Betty: "Are you from New Street, Pat and Lisa?"

    ______________________________.

5. Is Pussy Holly's cat?

    ______________________________.

6. Are Mrs White and Mr Dilwyn kids?

    ______________________________.

7. Are they teachers?

    ______________________________.

8. Is Maxi Ben's brother?

    ______________________________.

9. Is Billy Molly's father?

    ______________________________.

10. Is St. Peter's School big?

    ______________________________.

Manfred Bojes: Grundwissen englische Grammatik – 5./6. Klasse
© Persen Verlag

Exercise 2	Can you make questions and answers?

Is Are	Gwen Molly McMuff Timmy Ben's cats Mr Dilwyn Pat and Lisa	black and white? a teacher? Betty's old teacher? from Cardiff? twelve? from Doodle Street?	No, he isn't. Yes, they are. Yes, she is. No, she isn't. No, they aren't. Yes, he is.

1. ____?

   ______________________.

2. ____?

   ______________________.

3. ____?

   ______________________.

4. ____?

   ______________________.

5. ____?

   ______________________.

6. ____?

   ______________________.

7. ____?

   ______________________.

© Persen Verlag

6. Fragen mit Fragewörtern

Die wichtigsten Fragewörter im Englischen sind:

Who ...?	**Wer ...?**
What ...?	**Was ...?**
Where ...?	**Wo/Wohin ...?**
How ...?	**Wie ...?**

Die Fragewörter stehen wie im Deutschen immer am Anfang einer Frage.

<u>Beispiele:</u>

Who are you?	I'm Emmy.
What is under the table?	A dog.
Where is Tom?	At school.
How old is he?	Thirteen.

Achtung: Wegen ihrer Ähnlichkeit mit den deutschen Wörtern werden *who* und *where* oft verwechselt.

Dieser kleine Spruch kann dir aber helfen:

Who heißt **wer** und ***where*** heißt **wo**,
das weiß doch jeder Englisch-Floh!

© Persen Verlag

Exercise 1	Who is it?

Complete the sentences, please.

1	2	3	4

Susie Swift	Danny Dark	Brian Bond	Tina Tucker
12	18	14	17
London	York	Manchester	Liverpool
tennis	computer games	playing the guitar	dancing

1. __________ is it?	It's Susie Swift.
__________ old is she?	She is 12.
__________ is she from?	She is from London.
__________ is her hobby?	Tennis.
2. _________ is it?	It's _____________ _____________.
_________ ______ is he?	_________ __________ 18.
_________ ______ ______ from?	________ _______ ________ York.
___________ _____ his hobby?	_______________ _____________.
3. ______________ ______ it?	_______ Brian Bond.
__________ ______ is ______?	________ ________ 14.
___________ _____ _____ ______?	_______ ______ ________ Manchester.
4. _________ _____ _____?	________ _________ _________ ____________.
_________ ______ ___ _____?	________ _____ 17.
___________ ___ _____ from?	_______ ______ ______ ____________.
_________ ___ _____ _________?	Dancing.

© Persen Verlag

Exercise 2 — *Who*? or *Where*?

Look at exercise 1 again and complete the sentences.

1. _________ is 17? — Tina.
2. _________ is she from? — Liverpool.
3. _________ is Liverpool? — It is in England.
4. _________ is from London? — Susie.
5. _________ is Danny? — He is the boy from ____________.
6. _________ is Brian from? — He ___ ____ ________________.
7. _________ is 12? — _____________.
8. _________ is _________ from? — London.
9. _________ ____ London? — _____ _____ _____ England.
10. ______ _____ Tina? — ____ ___ ___ girl from _______________.

Manfred Bojes: Grundwissen englische Grammatik – 5./6. Klasse
© Persen Verlag

7. Der *s*-Genitiv und der *of*-Genitiv

Wenn du ausdrücken möchtest, dass etwas einer **Person** oder einem **Tier** gehört oder zugeordnet ist, benutzt du den *s*-Genitiv.
Dazu hängst du -*'s* an das betreffende Wort an.

> Beispiele:
>
> **Susie's** hobby is tennis.
> **Brian's** guitar is red.
> **The dog's** name is Bonzo.
> Tina is **Tom's** friend.

Bei Wörtern im Plural (Mehrzahl), die ja schon ein -*s* am Ende haben, hängst du für den Genitiv nur noch einen Apostroph an.

> Beispiele:
>
> The **boys'** names are Brian and Danny.
> The **teachers'** room is behind the brown door.
> The **cats'** baskets are in the corner.
> My **parents'** car is old.

Wenn du ausdrücken möchtest, dass etwas zu einer **Sache** gehört,
verwendest du den *of*-Genitiv. Eigentlich müsste er „*of-the*-Genitiv" heißen, weil nach dem *of* noch *the* folgen muss.

> Beispiele:
>
> The school is at the end **of the** street.
> The teacher's room is at the back **of the** hall.
> January is the first month **of the** year.
> The windows **of the** car are dirty.

© Persen Verlag

Exercise 1	**Tina Tucker in Liverpool**

Is it -*'s*, *'* or s?

The teacher___ at Tina Tucker___ school are nice.

The teacher___ room is near her classroom. In winter Tina___ classroom is often cold.

Upstairs there are her brother____ and four more classroom____.

They are not so cold. The Tucker___ house is in Newcastle Road.

The Beatles'____ famous singer and guitar player John Lennon____ early

home is there, too.

Tina___ MP3 has lot___ of the group____ song___ on it.

You know, the girl___ hobby is dancing, and the Beatles__ song___

are good for dancing!

Exercise 2	**Tina's *of* or *'s*-quiz**

Tina has got a quiz for her little brother. Can you do the quiz, too?

Example:
the girls / fingers -------------- the girls' fingers
the table / legs -------------- the legs of the table

1. the cat / mouth ------------ ______________________
2. Dad / hobby ------------ ______________________
3. the morning / your birthday ------------ ______________________
4. my friends / bikes ------------ ______________________
5. the door / classroom ------------ ______________________

Manfred Bojes: Grundwissen englische Grammatik – 5./6. Klasse
© Persen Verlag

8. Die Possessivbegleiter

Die Possessivbegleiter verwendest du, wenn du sagen möchtest, wem etwas gehört oder auch zu wem etwas gehört.

Sie heißen so, weil sie ein Nomen begleiten. Das ist in der deutschen und englischen Sprache gleich. Daher brauchst du diese Wörter einfach nur wie Vokabeln zu lernen.

Dies sind die Possesivbegleiter auf Englisch:

my – mein, meine
your – dein, deine, **I**hr, **I**hre
his – sein, seine
her – ihr, ihre
its – sein, seine, ihr, ihre (für Sachen und „namenlose" Tiere)
our – unser, unsere
your – euer, eure, **I**hr, **I**hre
their – ihr, ihre

Your kann also „dein" oder „euer" heißen. Wenn man jemanden siezt, kann es auch „Ihr" oder „Ihre" bedeuten.

Beispiele:

My name is Brian.
Your teacher is nice.
His sister is twelve.
Her name is Lucy.
Its rooms are small.
Our house is not big.
Your shirts are new.
Their dogs are young.

Lerntipp:
Folgende Wörter kann man leicht verwechseln, weil sie die gleiche oder eine ähnliche Aussprache haben:

your mit *you're* (du bist, ihr seid)
their mit *they're* (sie sind) und mit *there* (da, dort)

Wenn du dir nicht sicher bist, welches der Wörter gemeint ist, achte auf den Zusammenhang, in dem es gebraucht wird.

© Persen Verlag

Exercise 1	Brian Bond

Put in: *my – your – his – her – its – our – their*

Hi, ______ name is Brian. I'm from Manchester.

This is ______ house. ______ colour is grey, and ______ rooms are really large.

This is ______ sister. ______ name is Lucy.

Hey, Lucy, ______ MP3 is on the floor!

And this is my brother. ______ name is Harry.

Harry, ______ friend Olly is at the door.

Here are ______ dogs. ______ names are Rocky and Lucky.

Hey, Lucky and Rocky. ______ meal is ready!

Exercise 2	Right or wrong?

Put ticks.

		Right	wrong
Brian:	1. My sister's name is Lucy.	☐	☐
	2. Olly is her friend.	☐	☐
	3. The house is white and its doors are grey.	☐	☐
	4. Our name is Pond.	☐	☐
	5. Harry is my brother.	☐	☐
	6. His MP3 is on the floor.	☐	☐
	7. These are our cats. Their names are Rocky and Lucky.	☐	☐
	8. Look at Lucky and Rocky: their meal is ready.	☐	☐

© Persen Verlag

*Exercise 3	Olly at the Bonds' house

Put in: *my – your – our – their*

Olly: Hi, Brian and Harry. Aren't _______ parents at home?

Harry: No, they aren't. But _______ dogs are here.

Brian: _______ names are Lucky and Rocky.

Olly: I know. Oh, they're in _______ little dog house.

Harry: Look, Lucky and Rocky: what have I got?

Lucky and Rocky: Woof! Woof!

Harry: Okay, okay here are ________ dog biscuits.

Olly: Oh, and where are ________ biscuits? I like biscuits, too!

*Exercise 4	Brian's room is a mess.

Put in: *there – they – their – there – it's – there – its*

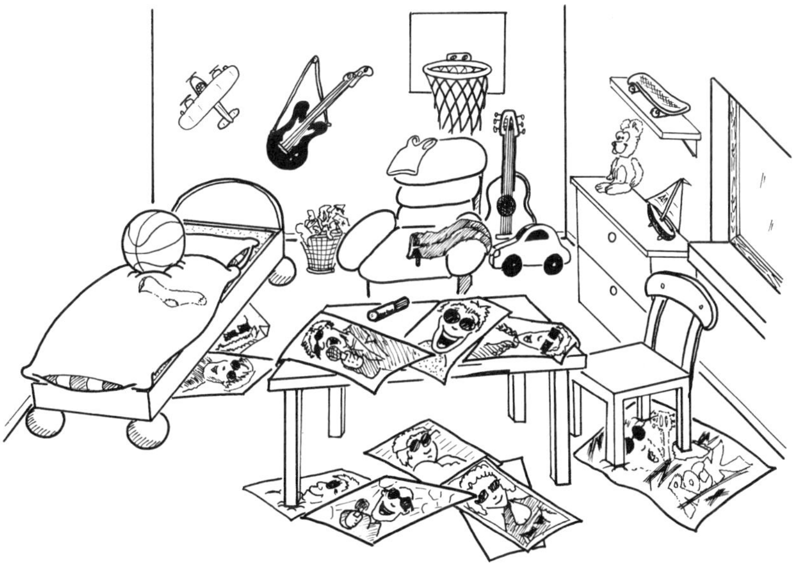

_______ are a lot of pop star photos in Brian's room. _______ are on the table, under the table und under the bed. Look at the stars: _______ are glasses on all _______ faces from Olly's magic marker! And what's that under the chair? _______ a big poster. _______ colours are pale and grey and _________ is a hole in it.

© Persen Verlag

9. *have got* und *has got*

Willst du ausdrücken, dass jemand etwas besitzt, kannst du *have got* bzw. *has got* verwenden.

Beispiele:

I have got a new bag.
You have got a small room.
He has got a sister.
She has got a baby brother.
Our house? It has got two doors.
We have got a nice teacher.
They have got three cats.

Wie du siehst, sagt man bei den Personen *he, she, it* ***has got***.

Lerntipp:
Du kannst dir an dieser Stelle schon einen hilfreichen Spruch merken:

***He, she, it* – das „s“ muss mit.**

Du wirst ihn später noch oft anwenden können!

Auch für *have got* und *has got* gibt es Kurzformen, die vor allem beim Sprechen benutzt werden.

Langform	Kurzform
I have got	I've got
you have got	you've got
he, she, it has got	he's, she's, it's got
we have got	we've got
you have got	you've got
they have got	they've got
I have not got	I haven't got
you have not got	you haven't got
he, she, it has not got	he, she, it hasn't got
we have not got	we haven't got
you have not got	you haven't got
they have not got	they haven't got

Auf Fragen mit *have got / has got* kannst du ähnlich wie bei *to be* Kurzantworten geben. Dabei lässt du *got* einfach weg.

Beispiele:

Have I got my money?	Yes, you have.	No, you haven't.
Have you got a bike?	Yes, I have.	No, I haven't.
Has Jack got a friend?	Yes, he has.	No, he hasn't.
Has Lara got a sister?	Yes, she has.	No, she hasn't.
Has your room got two chairs?	Yes, it has.	No, it hasn't.
Have we got a new teacher?	Yes, we have.	No, we haven't.
Have you got computers?	Yes, we have.	No, we haven't.
Have they got an old house?	Yes, they have.	No, they haven't.

© Persen Verlag

Exercise 1 — Susie Swift

Put in: *have got – has got*

Hi, I'm Susie Swift from London. We ____________ ______ a flat in Brandon Road. It ____________ ______ two small children's bedrooms. My parents ____________ ______ a big room. I ____________ ______ a room with my sister, Mary. She ____________ ______ a lot of T-shirts, so our wardrobe is often in a mess. And you? ____________ you ______ a sister or a brother?

*Exercise 2 — In the classroom

Put in: *have got – has got – is – are*

1. Who ____________ my ruler?

You ____________ it. Look, it ____________ in your bag.

2. We ____________ two new boys in our class. They ____________ from Luton, and they ____________ nice names: Lennox and Joshua.

3. Here ____________ my new pen. Look, it ____________ my name on it.

4. Oh, you ____________ a mascot!

Yes, he ____________ cool. He ____________ a funny name: Tiger!

5. Look, Tom and Olly. They ____________ a new comic.

Oh, yes, I know. It ____________ interesting; it ____________ really crazy pictures.

Exercise 3 — A fantasy interview with an alien

Complete the answers, please.

1. Have you got a brother or a sister? No, ______________________.
2. Have you got a mascot? Yes, ______________________.
3. Has it got a name? No, ______________________.
4. Have you got a friend? Yes, ____________. His name is Folo.
5. Has he got a UFO? No, ______________________.
6. Have you aliens got a lot of UFOs on your star? Yes, ______________.
7. Have your parents got funny antennas, too? Yes, ______________.
8. Have they got big feet, too? No, ______________.

*Exercise 4 — You and your family

Now write six or seven sentences about you and your family.
You can look for help in exercise 1–3.

Use: *have got – haven't got – has got – hasn't got*

____

____

____

____

____

____

____

____

____

© Persen Verlag

10. Das Hilfsverb *can/can't*

Sicher weißt du schon aus dem Deutschen, dass ein Hilfsverb nicht alleine steht, sondern zusammen mit einem anderen Verb benutzt wird.
Im Englischen ist ***can*** neben *to be* ein wichtiges Hilfsverb. Mit ihm und dem darauf folgenden Verb kannst du ausdrücken, was jemand **tun kann** oder auch **tun darf**.

Die Anwendung von ***can*** ist sehr einfach:
Can **bleibt** in allen Personen **unverändert,** und **auch das folgende Verb** bleibt immer **unverändert in seiner Grundform** stehen.

Beispiele:

I can see Tina in the garden.
You can call her.
Tina can dance.
The song can be fast or slow.

Die verneinte Form lautet ***cannot***, ihre Kurzform ***can't***. Beim Schreiben benutzt man meistens ***cannot***. Es wird zusammengeschrieben.

Beispiele:

I can't see Harry in the garden.
You cannot open a car without a key.
Tina cannot dance without music.
We can't see you, Lucy. Where are you?

Bei Kurzantworten mit *can/can't* wird das darauf folgende Verb einfach weggelassen.

Beispiele:

Can you help me, please?	– Yes, we can.
Can your brother play the guitar?	– No, he can't.
Can I have your bike, Mum?	– Yes, you can.
Can your friends play the guitar?	– No, they can't.

© Persen Verlag

Exercise 1 — What can they do?

	Tina	Harry	Lucy
make pizza	✗	✓	✗
dance	✓	✗	✓
play basketball	✗	✓	✗
read German	✓	✗	✓

Write down what they can do (✓) and what they cannot do (✗).

1. Tina ______________________________ make pizza.

   She ______________________________.

   She ______________________________.

   ______________________________.

2. Harry ______________________________.

   He ______________________________ dance.

   He ______________________________.

   ______________________________.

3. Lucy ______________________________.

   She ______________________________.

   She ______________________________.

   ______________________________ read German.

Manfred Bojes: Grundwissen englische Grammatik – 5./6. Klasse
© Persen Verlag

Exercise 2	*Can* or *can't*?

Put in: *he – she – they + can – can't*

1. Can Emily draw? Yes, _____ _______.

   Can she speak German? No, _____ _______.

2. Can Pinky and Punky write? Yes, _____ _______.

   Can they make pizza? No, _____ _______.

3. Can Barky spell? No, _____ _______.

   Can he make dog music? Yes, _____ _______.

4. Can Pussy read comics? No, _____ _______.

   Can she listen to music? Yes, _____ _______.

5. Can Boyboy play football? Yes, _____ _______.

   Can he see Pussy? No, _____ _______.

© Persen Verlag

11. Die einfache Gegenwart I (*simple present*)

Wenn du ausdrücken möchtest, dass etwas häufig oder regelmäßig passiert, verwendest du die einfache Gegenwart (*simple present*).

Beispiele:

I often go for a walk in the evening.
We always play tennis on Wednesday.
You read German books in your holidays.
Tina and Lucy dance every weekend.

Diese Zeitform benutzt du auch, wenn du eine allgemeingültige Aussage machen möchtest.

Beispiele:

I play the guitar.
You read comics.
They play computer games.
We like pop music.

Schließlich kannst du die einfache Gegenwart einsetzen, um zu beschreiben, dass mehrere Handlungen aufeinanderfolgen.

Beispiele:

First they go to Brian's house. Then they walk into the garden.
They look at the flowers. After that they have tea in the kitchen.

Wie du siehst, hat das Verb im *simple present* bei den meisten Personen, nämlich bei *I, you, we* und *they,* die gleiche Form wie der Infinitiv (die Grundform).

Manfred Bojes: Grundwissen englische Grammatik – 5./6. Klasse
© Persen Verlag

Exercise 1	**Three weeks**

Can you find the right verbs for the sentences?

Ricky

Use: *have – buy – meet – say*

1. On Mondays I ______________ my friend Rocky.
2. On Thursdays I ______________ food for my dog.
3. On Fridays I ______________ hello to my girlfriend Sarah.
4. On Saturdays we ______________ a good time at the disco together.

Sarah

Use: *get – enjoy – go out – cook*

1. On Tuesdays I ______________ pizza for my family from the snack.
2. On Wednesdays they ______________ a nice meal for me.
3. On Fridays I ______________ with my boyfriend Ricky.
4. On Saturdays we ______________ our time at the disco.

Pinky & Punky

Use: *take – say – go – visit*

1. On Mondays we __________ to work together.
2. Pinky: "On Tuesdays you __________ me on a motorbike ride, Punky."
3. Punky: "On Fridays we __________ Pinky's parents."
4. They __________: "You have got a crazy hairstyle, Punky!"

© Persen Verlag

Exercise 2	**A busy day for Mrs Swift**

Write the sentences in the right order.
Write the 12 verbs in a different colour, please.

I take the shopping home, and later on I pick up my neighbour and we go jogging in the park.

Then I take my neighbour home, go to school again and collect the kids.

After breakfast I take the children to school.

After dinner we watch a TV programme or read a book.

First I make breakfast in the morning.

After that I do the shopping because the supermarket is near the school.

Then they have dinner together with me because the kids are hungry after school.

Manfred Bojes: Grundwissen englische Grammatik – 5./6. Klasse
© Persen Verlag

12. Die einfache Gegenwart II – 3. Person Singular (*simple present – 3rd person singular*)

Du hast bereits gelernt, dass bei den Personen *I*, *you*, *we*, *you* und *they* das *simple present* ganz einfach gebildet wird: Man benutzt nur die Grundform des Verbs (Infinitiv).

Bei der 3. Person Singular, also **bei *he, she, it*, wird noch ein „s" an die Grundform angehängt**.

Lerntipp:
Oder anders ausgedrückt:

***He, she, it* – das „s" muss mit.**

Beispiele:

He plays the guitar. She reads German books.
This is our house, it looks new.
Mrs Swift makes breakfast in the morning.
Ricky buys food for his dog.
A big dog eats a lot of dog biscuits.

Wenn ein Verb in seiner Grundform mit einem Zischlaut endet, z. B. mit „***-sh***" oder „***-ch***", hängst du an die Grundform ***-es*** an.

Beispiele:

Mrs Swift watches a TV programme with her children.
Mrs White teaches English and German at school.
Ricky finishes his homework in the evening.

Auch die Verben ***do*** und ***go*** erhalten bei ***he, she, it*** ein ***-es*** angehängt.

Beispiele:

Mrs Swift does the shopping. She goes jogging in the park.
Ricky goes out on Fridays. Punky does his work together with Pinky.

Wenn ein Verb auf **-y endet und vor dem *y* ein Mitlaut (Konsonant) steht**, ist die Endung bei *he, she, it* ***-ies***.

Beispiele:

She carries a box.
The bird flies away.

© Persen Verlag

*Exercise 1	Ron's week

Don't forget to use ***-s****,* ***-es*** *or* ***-ies****.*

a) *Put in:* *start – have – watch – come – go*

1. He ______________ to work by bike.

2. His work ______________ at 7.45.

3. He ______________ lunch at 12.30.

4. He ______________ home at 18.00.

5. He ______________ TV after 20.15.

b) *Put in:* *play – carry – do – finish – wash*

1. On Wednesdays he ______________ a basket full of dirty clothes to the bathroom and ______________ his clothes in an old washing machine.

2. On Thursdays he ______________ his homework for a computer evening class.

3. On Fridays his work ______________ at 3.30 in the afternoon.

4. On Saturdays he ______________ football with his friend Ricky.

Manfred Bojes: Grundwissen englische Grammatik – 5./6. Klasse
© Persen Verlag

Exercise 2	**Hobbies**

a) ***s*** *or not? Put the sentences together and put an* ***s*** *to the verbs where necessary.*

1. play – Ron and Ricky – football

   ____.

2. Mrs Swift – in the park – go jogging

   ____.

3. a lot of dog biscuits – like – Ricky's dog

   ____.

4. read books – the Swifts – and – watch TV

   ____.

5. enjoy – Sarah – her time at the disco.

   ____.

6. Pinky and Punky – go – on a motorbike ride.

   ____.

*b) *Write five sentences about your friends' and family's hobbies, please.*

1. ____.
2. ____.
3. ____.
4. ____.
5. ____.

© Persen Verlag

13. Die Satzstellung in der einfachen Gegenwart

In englischen Aussagesätzen gilt für die Satzstellung diese Reihenfolge:

Subjekt – Verb – Objekt

Beispiele:

I	like	football.
He	can play	the guitar.
They	have got	a black car.

Wenn du in einem Satz Zeitangaben machen möchtest, kannst du sie an den **Anfang oder an das Ende** des Satzes stellen.

Beispiele:

In the morning I clean my teeth. I clean my teeth **in the morning**.
On Sundays we go for a walk. We go for a walk **on Sundays**.

Die Zeitangabe wird stärker betont, wenn sie am Anfang steht.

Ortsangaben stellst du am besten **an das Ende**.

Beispiele:

He puts the clothes **into the washing machine**.
We play football **behind the school**.

Möchtest du eine Orts- und eine Zeitangabe machen, hast du zwei Möglichkeiten:

Du stellst die Zeitangabe nach vorn und die Ortsangabe an das Ende, oder du setzt beide Angaben an das Ende. Dann gilt aber: **Ort vor Zeit**, d. h. erst kommt die Ortsangabe und dann die Zeitangabe.

Beispiele:

Every Thursday he puts his clothes **into the washing machine.**
He puts his clothes **into the washing machine every Thursday**.
On Saturdays they go jogging **in the park**.
They go jogging **in the park on Saturdays**.

© Persen Verlag

Häufigkeitsadverbien wie

always = immer, *often* = oft, *never* = nie,
sometimes = manchmal, *usually* = normalerweise

werden oft zusammen mit der einfachen Gegenwart (*simple present*) verwendet.

Sie werden daher auch **„Signalwörter"** genannt, weil sie dir das Signal geben, beim Gebrauch dieser Wörter das *simple present* zu verwenden.

Die Häufigkeitsadverbien haben ihren Platz **zwischen Subjekt und Verb.**

Beispiele:

I **always** get up at 7.15.
My mother **sometimes** takes me to school by car.
The Swifts **often** watch TV in the evening.
We **usually** go to bed at 21.15.

Wenn eine Form von *to be* im Satz steht, setzt du das Häufigkeitsadverb **hinter die Form von *to be***.

Beispiele:

Our teacher **is sometimes** late.
We **are often** tired.
I **am never** angry.

Wenn ein anderes Hilfsverb wie *can* oder *must* im Satz steht, setzt du das **Häufigkeitsadverb immer hinter das Hilfsverb.**

Beispiele:

You **can always** come.
We **must never** shout.
Mrs White **can sometimes** get angry.

© Persen Verlag

Exercise 1	**Sarah's mix 4 you**

a) This is Sarah's mix about her week. Can you put the words in the right order?

1. at the snack bar – buy pizza – often – I – on Tuesdays

   ____.

2. a nice meal for us – my mother – on Sundays – cooks – usually

   ____.

3. On Fridays – can – with Ricky – I – sometimes – go to the disco

   ____.

4. I – with my teddy mascot – every evening – go to bed

   ____.

b) Here is Sarah's mix about Ron. Can you put these words in the right order, too?

1. usually – every Monday – his friend Ron sees – he

   ____.

2. On Thursdays – sometimes – he – to the pet shop – must – go

   ____.

3. me – on Fridays – he – meets – always

   ____.

4. he – never – on Tuesdays – goes – to the disco with me

   ____.

© Persen Verlag

*Exercise 2	Sandra in Germany

Susie's friend Sandra is at a German school in Köln for a few weeks.
She writes to Susie on facebook. But something is wrong with her computer.

Hi Susie,
School is very different here. We ++++++ up at 6.45 (usually). We ++++++ to school by bus (always). Then we ++++++ to Lena's friends on the bus (often). School ++++++ at 7.45 (always). You ++++++ at school then (never)!

We ++++++ sweets at a little tuck shop near the school (sometimes). They ++++++ school at 1.30 (usually). That's great! It's a very good idea for our school, too.

Bye for now, Sandra

Can you write Sandra's text and put the adverbs in their place?

Use these verbs: *start – finish – buy – get up – talk – be – go*

Hi Susie,

School is very different here. We ____________________

____

____

____

____

____

____

That's great! It's a very good idea for our school, too.

Bye for now, Sandra.

© Persen Verlag

*Exercise 3 | Mediation

Lena aus Köln ist für eine Woche bei Sandra in London. Sandras Eltern möchten den Klang der deutschen Sprache kennenlernen. Daher erzählt Lena auf Deutsch von ihrer Familie und Sandra übersetzt, weil sie schon gut deutsch versteht.

Lena

Wir wohnen in Köln-Porz. Mein Vater arbeitet an einer Schule. Meine Mutter fährt jeden Tag eine Stunde mit dem Bus zur Arbeit. Sie arbeitet in einem Computerladen.
Nach der Schule mag ich frische Luft. Dann nehme ich meinen kleinen Bruder Jakob oft mit in den Park. Er bellt alle Hunde an und fragt sie dann: „Wuff, ich kann bellen. Aber kannst du auch sprechen?"

Sandra

They ____________________ Köln-Porz. Her father

____.

Her mother _________________________________

____.

She ______________________________ computer

shop. After school ____________________________

fresh air. Then she ____________________________

____.

____

____

____.

Manfred Bojes: Grundwissen englische Grammatik – 5./6. Klasse
© Persen Verlag

14. Der Imperativ (Befehlsform)

Mit der Befehlsform, also dem Imperativ, kannst du jemanden bitten oder auffordern, etwas zu tun oder gerade nicht zu tun. Auch eine Warnung kannst du mit dieser Form ausdrücken.

Meistens steht am Anfang oder Ende eines Satzes das Wort *please.* Wenn es fehlt, kann das unhöflich wirken.

Für die Bildung der Befehlsform benutzt du die Grundform des Verbs, und zwar ohne *to.* Dabei ist es egal, ob du eine Person oder mehrere Personen ansprichst.

Beispiele:

Please help me with my homework.
Put the book into the box, please.
Open the window, please.
Listen, there is a thunderstorm.

Willst du jemanden auffordern oder bitten, etwas nicht zu tun, setzt du einfach *don't* vor die Grundform des Verbs.

Beispiele:

Please don't write in your Maths books.
Don't shout in the classroom, please.
Don't clean your bike in the house.

© Persen Verlag

Exercise 1	**Rules at the Bakers' house**

Write down the rules, please.

a) Rules for Tim.

	do	your sister.
	take	your room.
Please	clean	your homework.
	help	your bed.
	make	the dog for a walk.

____.

____.

____.

____.

____.

b) Rules for Tim's parents.

	call	my emails,	
	take away	my room without knocking,	
Don't	walk into	on my mobile,	please.
	play	with my mascot,	
	read	my basketball,	

____.

____.

____.

____.

____.

Manfred Bojes: Grundwissen englische Grammatik – 5./6. Klasse
© Persen Verlag

Exercise 2	School rules

a) *Put the words in the right order, please.*

1. late / be / don't

______________________________________.

2. to the teachers / say / Please / "good morning"

______________________________________.

3. eat and drink / please / Don't / in the classroom,

______________________________________.

4. Listen / please / to the teachers,

______________________________________.

5. on the stairs / don't / run

______________________________________.

*b) *Write down five more rules for school, please.*

1. ______________________________________.

2. ______________________________________.

3. ______________________________________.

4. ______________________________________.

5. ______________________________________.

© Persen Verlag

Exercise 3	**Signs**

What do the signs say?

Here's some help:

*sit – take photos – eat – take in your dog here –
smoke – drink the water – walk – use a mobile*

1. ______________________________

2. ______________________________

3. ______________________________

4. ______________________________

5. ______________________________

6. ______________________________

7. ______________________________

8. ______________________________

Manfred Bojes: Grundwissen englische Grammatik – 5./6. Klasse
© Persen Verlag

15. Die Personalpronomen (Objektformen)

Du kennst schon die Personalpronomen *I, you, he, she, it, we, you* und *they*. Sie drücken aus, wer etwas tut. Neben diesen Subjektformen gibt es auch **Objektformen**, die angeben, **auf wen sich eine Handlung bezieht**.

Im Deutschen gibt es bei den Objektpronomen oft mehrere Formen, z. B. *mir/mich*, *dir/dich* oder *ihn/ihm*. Im Englischen brauchst du dagegen für jede Person nur eine Form zu lernen.

Subjektform	Objektform		
I	me		mir/mich
you	you		dir/dich
		Als Anrede:	Ihnen/Sie
he	him		ihm/ihn
she	her		ihr/sie
it	it		ihm/es
we	us		uns
you	you		euch
		Als Anrede:	Ihnen/Sie
they	them		ihnen/sie

Das Objektpronomen steht im Englischen immer hinter dem Vollverb.

Beispiele:

Can you drive **me** to the hockey club, Dad?
I can give **you** the address.
There's Ron. Go with **him**. I can give **him** the car key.
Where is Mum? I can't see **her**.
Oh, a butterfly. Can you see **it**, Sophie?
Dad often takes **us** to school by car.
Tim and Sophie, can we leave **you** alone at home?
The kids are OK. You can leave **them** at home.

© Persen Verlag

Exercise 1	**A bus ticket**

Put in: *you – me – it*

1. Sophie: "I want to go the zoo. Can you give ________ your bus ticket?"
2. Tim: "Oh, sorry, I can't give ________ my ticket. I haven't got ________ here at home. It's in my hockey bag at school."
3. Sandra: "Can ________ drive ________ to school today, Dad? I'm late."

Exercise 2	**A new programme**

Put in: *you – us – it*

Here are the two rap DJs from Radio York! You can listen to ________ every day.

And when you phone ________, we listen to ________ and play your requests.

Today we start our new hip hop programme.

Listen to ________, phone ________ and say if you like ________ or not.

Manfred Bojes: Grundwissen englische Grammatik – 5./6. Klasse
© Persen Verlag

Exercise 3	**At the zoo**

Put in: *him – them*

Oh, there are two white kangaroos. Look at __________.

And here's a zookeeper, he must clean their cage. Let's watch __________.

And look, there are two sticks in the water near the kangaroos' cage.

We can take __________ and play hockey with __________.

Exercise 4	**Tim's and Sophie's cousin**

Put in: *me – you – her – it – them*

Chloe wants to visit the Bakers in York.

Her cousins Tim and Sophie live there.

She wants to visit __________. But where's the street?

It is on her map, but she can't really find __________.

Can a policewoman help __________?

Chloe: "Excuse __________, can you help __________ to find

Adelaide Street, please?"

Policewoman: "Of course I can help __________. Look, here it is very small on your map. Can you see __________?"

© Persen Verlag

Exercise 5	**Tim, Sophie and Chloe in York**

Put in: *me – you – him – it – us – them*

a) Sophie: Tim, let's fly our kite. Can _______ help me with _______?

Tim: I'm sorry, I can't help _______ just now. Look, there is Dad.

You can ask _______.

An hour later.

b) Chloe: Sophie, where are the photos of _______ in Germany?

Can I see _______, please?

Sophie: Look, this is a photo of _______ and Mum.

It's a nice photo of _______.

Sophie: Hey, there is Dad! Talk to _______ in German,

not in English. He likes _______.

***Exercise 6**	**Helpful phrases in English**

Can you say the sentences in English?

Können Sie uns helfen?

____?

Können wir bei Ihnen übernachten?

____?

Das Zimmer ist klein, aber wir nehmen es.

____?

Unsere Koffer sind im Taxi, können wir sie hereinholen?

____?

© Persen Verlag

16. Frage und Verneinung mit *do* und *don't*

Du hast bisher Fragen im Englischen genau wie im Deutschen gestellt.

Beispiele:

Can Mr Baker speak German?	Kann Mr Baker deutsch sprechen?
Is he from York?	Ist er aus York?
Are you eleven?	Bist du elf?
Has Tim got a sister?	Hat Tim eine Schwester?

Du siehst, dass du immer ein Hilfsverb (*can, is, are, have/has …*) brauchst, wenn du eine Frage stellst. Aber was kannst du machen, wenn kein Hilfsverb vorhanden ist? Ganz einfach: Dann nimmst du das Hilfsverb ***do***.

Beispiele:

Do you like basketball?	Magst du Basketball?
Do the girls play hockey?	Spielen die Mädchen Hockey?
Do we meet our tutor on Mondays?	Treffen wir montags unseren Klassenlehrer?

Wenn du eine Kurzantwort geben möchtest, greifst du ***do*** in der Antwort wieder auf.

Beispiele:

Do you like basketball?	– Yes, I do. / No, I don't.
Do they play hockey?	– Yes, they do. / No, they don't.
Do we meet our tutor on Mondays?	– Yes, we do. / No, we don't.

Bei der Verneinung ist es genau wie bei der Frage:
Enthält ein Satz kein Hilfsverb, musst du ***don't*** einsetzen, wenn du etwas verneinen möchtest.

Beispiele:
I don't go to school by bus.
You don't like hockey.
We don't go to school on Saturdays.
The children don't meet their tutor on Mondays.
I can't sleep.
He isn't tired.

Auch bei Fragen mit Fragewörtern (*what, where, when, why, how*) brauchst du das Wörtchen *do*, falls kein Hilfsverb im Satz vorhanden ist.

Beispiele:

Where do you go on holiday?
What do they play at the weekends?
When do I meet the tutor?
Why do we always get so much homework?

Du siehst: Erst kommt das Fragewort, dann *do.*

© Persen Verlag

Exercise 1 | Jumbo and Skippy: an interview about kangaroos

Can you match the answers to the questions?

Do
you
you and your friends

play basketball?
like rap music?
watch animal DVDs?
eat flowers?
drink kangaroo lemonade?
have parties?

Yes, we do. You can come and dance with us.
No, I don't. I like the "Kick-And-Run" music!
Yes, I do, but only elephant films.
No, I don't. I drink elephant tail soup.
Yes, we do. Our team is "The Skippy All Stars".
Yes, we do if they are sweet.

Now write the correct questions and answers down, please.

Do ______________________________ basketball?

______________________________.

Do ______________________________ music?

______________________________.

______________________________ DVDs?

______________________________.

______________________________ flowers?

______________________________.

______________________________ lemonade?

______________________________.

______________________________ parties?

______________________________.

Manfred Bojes: Grundwissen englische Grammatik – 5./6. Klasse
© Persen Verlag

Exercise 2	Sophie's day

Chloe asks her cousin Sophie about her day.

Put in: *where – what – when – how – why*

1. __________ do you get up? – At half past seven.
2. __________ do you do then? – I have breakfast.
3. __________ do you have breakfast? – In the kitchen, of course.
4. __________ do you usually have for breakfast? – I often have muesli.

5. __________ do you go to school? – By bus.
6. __________ do you come back home? – At quarter past four.
7. __________ do you do after school? – I often take the neighbour's dog for a walk.
8. __________ do you go? – To Dean's Park.
9. __________ do you go to the park? – Because the dog likes the rabbits in the park.
10. __________ do you go to the park? – I often walk, but sometimes I go by bike and the dog must run.

© Persen Verlag

Exercise 3 | An interview with Tony Maroni

What
Where
When
Do
How

My name is Tony Maroni from Pisa.

Can you find out the question words?

1. *twah* is your name?
2. *rehew* do you live?
3. *nehw* do you get up?
4. *woh* do you go to school?
5. *od* you like your English teacher?
6. *reweh* do you have lunch?
7. *nehw* do you come home from school?
8. *hatw* are your hobbies?
9. *twah* do you do in the evenings?
10. *waht* songs do you listen to?
11. *who* old are your parents?

a) Yes, I do. She is nice.
b) My name is Tony Maroni.
c) They are 41 and 38.
d) I live in Pisa.
e) I listen to songs from Lady Gaga.
f) At quarter past seven.
g) I often ride my bike in the evenings.
h) By bike, of course.
i) Kissing my girlfriend and eating spaghetti.
j) I have lunch at home.
k) I come home from school at half past one.

Now write down the correct questions and the letter for the correct answer, please.

<u>Example:</u>
1. What is your name? b)

2. ____________________? ______
3. ____________________? ______
4. ____________________? ______
5. ____________________? ______
6. ____________________? ______
7. ____________________? ______
8. ____________________? ______
9. ____________________? ______
10. ____________________? ______
11. ____________________? ______

Manfred Bojes: Grundwissen englische Grammatik – 5./6. Klasse
© Persen Verlag

Exercise 4	What you like to do on your birthday

a) Here are things you can do on your birthday. Look at the pictures and write down things you like and things you don't like.

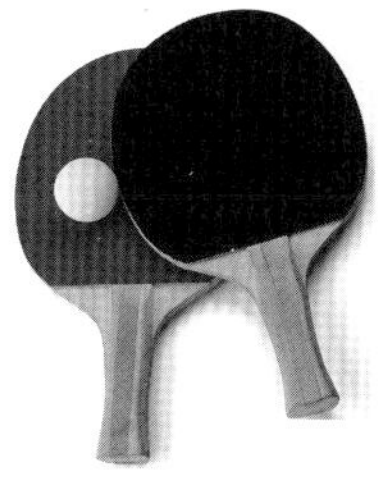

I like ______________________________.

______________________________.

______________________________.

______________________________.

I don't like ______________________________.

______________________________.

______________________________.

______________________________.

______________________________.

*b) Now write down two more things you like and two more things you don't like on your birthday.

____

____

____

© Persen Verlag

17. Frage und Verneinung mit *does* und *doesn't*

Du hast bereits gelernt, wie man Fragen und Verneinungen mit ***do*** bildet, wenn kein Hilfsverb im Satz ist.

In diesen Sätzen kamen nur die Personen *I, you, we, you* und *they* vor.

Wenn du Fragen und Verneinungen mit *he, she, it* bilden möchtest, kommt die bekannte Regel wieder zur Anwendung:

***He, she, it* – das „s" muss mit.**

Darum wird bei *he, she, it* und bei den Wörtern, die durch *he, she, it* ersetzt werden können, in Fragen und Verneinungen

do zu ***does***

und ***don't*** zu ***doesn't***.

Beispiele:

Does Mr Baker speak German? – Yes, he does.
Does he speak Spanish? – No, he doesn't.
Does Sophie get up at half past seven? – Yes, she does.
Does she go to school by bike? – No, she doesn't.
Does it always rain in York? – No, it doesn't.
Tony Maroni doesn't live in London.
He doesn't come home from school at 3 o'clock.
The sun doesn't always shine in Pisa.

Du siehst:
Wenn du ***does*** oder ***doesn't*** verwendest, darfst du an das Verb im Satz jetzt **kein *s* mehr** anhängen, weil es ja schon in ***does*** bzw. ***doesn't*** steckt.

Manfred Bojes: Grundwissen englische Grammatik – 5./6. Klasse
© Persen Verlag

Exercise 1	*Do* or *does*? – *Don't* or *doesn't*?

Complete the sentences, please.

1. ________ Billy like computers?

   Yes, ______________________.

2. ________ Mr Ping and Mr Pong like running?

   No, ______________________.

3. ________ Dr. Feelgood work with pets?

   No, ______________________.

4. ________ Stella and Don dance at the weekends?

   Yes, ______________________.

5. "________ you clean your teeth in the evenings, Timmy?"

   Yes, ______________________.

6. ________ the castle look new?

   No, ______________________.

7. ________ the people in the choir sing songs in the evening?

   Yes, ______________________.

8. ________ Pongo play table tennis after school?

   Yes, ______________________.

© Persen Verlag

*Exercise 2	Does he like it? Does she like it?

Make questions and answers.

<u>*Example:*</u>

Pit … bike trips? ☹ … mountain trips ☺

Does Pit like bike trips? No, he doesn't

Does he like mountain trips? Yes, he does.

1. Chuck … hamburgers? ☺ … cheeseburgers? ☹

____________________? ____________________.

____________________? ____________________.

2. Finn … swimming? ☹ … bike trips? ☺

____________________? ____________________.

____________________? ____________________.

3. Susie … her boyfriend? ☺ … hamsters? ☹

____________________? ____________________.

____________________? ____________________.

4. Robby … table tennis? ☺ … tennis? ☹

____________________? ____________________.

____________________? ____________________.

5. Chuck ... fast cars? ☹ … fast food? ☺

____________________? ____________________.

____________________? ____________________.

6. Paul … housework? ☺ … garden work? ☹

____________________? ____________________.

____________________? ____________________.

Manfred Bojes: Grundwissen englische Grammatik – 5./6. Klasse
© Persen Verlag

*Exercise 3	Tony Ticket's week

Can you find the questions about Tony's week? Write them down, please.
The underlined words can help you to find correct question words.

Use: *what – how – why – where – when*

1. ______________________________?

He lives <u>in Grimsby</u>.

2. ______________________________?

He gets up <u>at half past seven</u>.

3. ______________________________?

He gets to school <u>on his bike</u>.

4. ______________________________?

At five o'clock in the afternoon <u>he does his homework</u>.

5. ______________________________?

He goes to church <u>on Sundays</u>.

6. ______________________________?

He plays football <u>in the garden</u>.

7. ______________________________?

On Tuesdays <u>he goes swimming</u>.

8. ______________________________?

He likes Thursdays <u>because he can play in his music group.</u>

9. ______________________________?

He meets his girlfriend Peggy <u>on Fridays</u>.

10. ______________________________?

On Saturdays he goes <u>to the disco</u> with Peggy.

© Persen Verlag

Exercise 4	**Oh, that is wrong!**

Put in: *don't* or *doesn't*

1. The Burtons go shopping every day. – No, they __________ go shopping every day. They go to work every day.
2. Tim goes to bed with a map. – No, he __________ go to bed with a map, it's a mascot.
3. Their neighbour's dog sleeps in a picnic bag. – No, it __________ sleep in a picnic bag. It's a basket.
4. Children do their homework at school. – No, they usually __________ do it at school. They do it at home.
5. "Do you like long trips, Chloe?" – "No, I __________ like them. They're boring."
6. Sophie wakes Tim up in the morning. – No, she __________ wake him up. Tim has got an alarm clock.

***Exercise 5**	**It's your turn**

a) *Write down four things you don't do every day.*

1. ______________________________.
2. ______________________________.
3. ______________________________.
4. ______________________________.

b) *Now write down four things your mother or your father doesn't do every day.*

1. ______________________________.
2. ______________________________.
3. ______________________________.
4. ______________________________.

Manfred Bojes: Grundwissen englische Grammatik – 5./6. Klasse
© Persen Verlag

*Exercise 6	Find the questions.

Use: How does ...? – Does...? – When do ...? – Where does ...? – Where do ...? – Why does ...? – When do ...? – What does ...? – Why does ...?

1. ________ ________ Cilly and her dog go for a walk?
   In the evenings.

2. ________ ________ Pit go to the mountains?
   Because he likes them.

3. ________ ________ Tim often sleep ?
   In his tent.

4. ________ ________ Razy like garden work?
   No, he doesn't like it.

5. ________ ________ Sam do when he sees a monster?
   He runs away.

6. ________ ________ Fiona and Joan go surfing?
   Every Friday.

7. ________ ________ Chuck go on a holiday trip?
   By car.

8. ________ ________ Pit and Pat go on Saturdays?
   To the tennis club.

9. ________ ________ Clexy work with colours?
   Because it's his job.

© Persen Verlag

18. Die Demonstrativpronomen *this – that / these – those*

Das Wort ***this*** weist auf etwas hin, das sich in deiner Nähe befindet. Man kann es mit „dieser/diese/dies hier" übersetzen. *This* wir häufig zusammen mit *here* verwendet.

Mit ***that*** weist du auf etwas hin, das weiter entfernt ist. Man kann es mit „der/die/das da" oder „der/die/das dort hinten" übersetzen.
Es wird oft zusammen mit „*over there*" verwendet.

Beispiele:

This is my baby brother here.	Dies hier ist mein kleiner Bruder.
And that is my Dad over there.	Und das da ist mein Papa.
This is our car and that car behind the fence is our neighbours' car.	Dies hier ist unser Auto und das dort hinter dem Zaun ist das Auto unserer Nachbarn.

Wenn du Personen oder Sachen einander gegenüberstellst, sagst du zuerst *this* und danach *that*, auch dann, wenn beide gleich weit entfernt sind.

Beispiele:

This is my sister and that is my brother.	Dies ist meine Schwester und das ist mein Bruder.
This is a map of Britain and that is a map of Germany.	Dies ist eine Karte von Großbritannien und das ist eine Deutschlandkarte.

This und *that* gebrauchst du, wenn du auf jeweils eine Person oder einen Gegenstand hinweist (Einzahl). Wenn du auf mehrere Personen oder Gegenstände hinweisen möchtest, verwendest du für die Mehrzahl statt *this* das Wort ***these***. Die Mehrzahl für *that* ist ***those***.

Beispiele:

These are my new toys here and those are my new books over there.	Dies hier sind meine neuen Spielsachen und das da sind meine neuen Bücher.
These are Tim's pullovers and those are Susie's pullovers.	Dies sind Tims Pullover und das sind Susies Pullover.
These are new socks and those are old socks.	Dies sind neue Socken und das sind alte Socken.

Manfred Bojes: Grundwissen englische Grammatik – 5./6. Klasse
© Persen Verlag

Exercise 1 | Here → Over there

Put in: *this – that* *these – those*

______ girl is a computer programmer, … → … and ______ man is a doctor.

______ people are in a choir, … → … and ______ people are at work.

______ people like to dance, … → … and ______ woman likes the mountains.

______ man's hobby is his bike, … → … and ______ boys' hobby are hamburgers.

______ people are on holiday, … → … and ______ man is in his garden.

______ boys are on ice-skates, … → … and ______ people are on a blanket.

© Persen Verlag

Exercise 2 | In the classroom

Put in: *this – that – these – those*

1. __________ is my biro here and __________ is Tim's biro over there.
2. __________ is my sandwich here and __________ is Tim's sandwich over there.
3. __________ is Sheila's jacket near the door and __________ is her cap here.
4. __________ are my folders here and __________ are the teacher's folders on his desk.
5. __________ are Henry's exercise books on his table and __________ are my neighbour's here.
6. __________ are posters and __________ are photos.
7. __________ is our timetable and __________ is our plan for the class tests.
8. __________ keys on the teacher's desk are Mr Dixon's keys; __________ keys in my hand are my keys.
9. Here are apples from the school tuck shop; let's eat one of __________ apples.
10. __________ isn't my school blazer over there on the stand, __________ is my blazer over my chair.
11. __________ are Tim's friends at the door and __________ is my friend Jack here.
12. __________ here aren't my felt pens, but isn't __________ yellow felt pen on your table one of my pens?

© Persen Verlag

19. Die Verlaufsform der Gegenwart I *(present progressive)*

Du kennst bereits die einfache Gegenwart (*simple present*), mit der du ausdrücken kannst, dass etwas häufig oder regelmäßig passiert.

Mit der Verlaufsform der Gegenwart beschreibst du etwas, das **gerade geschieht** und noch nicht zu Ende ist.

Die einfache Formel für die Bildung dieser Zeitform lautet:

am/is/are* + Verb + *ing

Ob du *am, is,* oder *are* verwendest, hängt von der Personalform ab, die du nennst (z. B.: *I am, you are, he is, we are, they are*).

Beispiele:

I **am listening** to my favourite song now. It **is raining** at the moment.
She **is** just **reading** her book. The man **is sitting** in the taxi.
Look, they **are coming** out of their house. Listen, they **are singing**.

Du findest in den Beispielsätzen die Wörter *now, just, at the moment, look* und *listen*, die hier häufig gebraucht werden. Sie wirken wie Signale, die anzeigen, dass man die Verlaufsform verwenden muss. Sie werden daher auch oft als **Signalwörter** bezeichnet.

An den Beispielen siehst du auch, dass sich die Schreibung von Verben bei der Verlaufsform der Gegenwart ändern kann, z. B. *com~~e~~* → *coming* und *sit* → *sitting*.

Hier gelten folgende Regeln:
1. Bei Verben mit einem stummen, also nicht gesprochenen -*e* am Ende entfällt das -*e*.

2. Bei Verben, die mit einem Konsonanten (Mitlaut) enden und davor einen kurzen Vokal (Selbstlaut) haben, verdoppelt sich der Endkonsonant.

Beispiele:

The bus driver is **driving** a green bus. I am **writing** an email.
The kids are **swimming** in the lake. Sheila is just **putting** her books into her bag.

© Persen Verlag

Exercise 1	Saturday morning in Keswick

It is Saturday morning in Keswick in the Lake District. What are the people doing?

Complete the sentences and use the present progressive of these verbs:

make – have – listen – swim – play – clean – drive – dance – ride – go

1. Olivia ______________________________ in the pool.

2. Rob and Bob ______________________________ the car.

3. Dusty ______________________________ his horse.

4. Paul and Sue ______________________________.

5. Ben Quick ______________________________ an interview for his TV programme.

6. Bonzo ______________________________ with two balls.

7. Herbie ______________________________ to his ghetto blaster.

8. Pinky and Punky ______________________________ for a walk.

9. Mr Shane ______________________________ his taxi.

10. Mr and Mrs Sleepy ______________________________ breakfast.

Manfred Bojes: Grundwissen englische Grammatik – 5./6. Klasse
© Persen Verlag

*Exercise 2	Saturday afternoon in Keswick

What are the people in Keswick doing?
Use the present progressive of one of the two verbs in brackets.

<u>Example:</u>

Doris and Danny (dance/sleep)
are dancing at the disco.

1. Stiffy (sit/teach) ____________________ on his bike.

2. Becky (read/write) ____________________ a book.
3. Stella, Lobo, Tony and Bobo (read/sing) ________________ a song.

4. Ronny (do/wash) ____________________ his homework.
5. Holly and Molly (play/run) ____________________ to the bus stop.
6. John (visit/teach) ____________________ his girlfriend.

7. Beefy (eat/clean) ____________________ a hamburger.
8. A lot of people (take/watch) ____________________ a football match.
9. Robby (phone/help) ____________________ his mum.

10. Pit: "I (have/talk) ____________________ a good time at the lake."

© Persen Verlag

20. Die Verlaufsform der Gegenwart II (*present progressive*)

Wenn du Fragen mit der Verlaufsform der Gegenwart (*present progressive*) stellen möchtest, kannst du sie, wie du bereits gelernt hast, mit dem Hilfsverb bilden.

Du beginnst die Frage also entweder mit *Am ...?*, *Is ...?* oder *Are ...?*
oder mit einem Fragewort (*who, what, where, when, why, how many ...)*, an das sich *am, is*, oder *are* sofort anschließt.

Wie du schon gelernt hast, kann es unhöflich klingen, wenn du eine Frage nur mit *yes* oder *no* beantwortest. Du kannst in solchen Fällen besser einen verkürzten Satz, also eine Kurzantwort bilden.

Beispiele:

Am I in the right classroom?	– Yes, you are.
Are you talking to me?	– No, I'm not.
Is he asking me?	– No, he isn't.
Are we making a noise?	– Yes, you are.
Are they drinking water?	– No, they aren't.

Who am I listening to?	– You're listening to your new tutor.
Where are you coming from?	– I'm coming from the Bakers'.
What is she doing here?	– She's repairing the printer.
Why isn't the sun shining?	– Because the weather is bad today.

Möchtest du die Verlaufsform verneinen, fügst du einfach *not* bzw. *n't* hinter *am, is*, oder *are* ein.

Beispiele:

I'm not going shopping.
You aren't eating your sandwich.
She isn't listening.
It is not raining.
We are not learning Spanish.
They aren't watching TV.

Es gibt nur einige wenige Verben, mit denen du keine Verlaufsform bilden kannst. Die wichtigsten sind: *can, want to* und *have got.*

Manfred Bojes: Grundwissen englische Grammatik – 5./6. Klasse
© Persen Verlag

Exercise 1	What are they doing in the city?

a) *Find out what the people in the pictures are doing.*

1. Four kids ______________________ school uniform.

2. Three men ______________________ big boxes.

3. A boy ______________________ a comic.

4. A woman ______________________ a taxi.

5. Two ladies ______________________ shopping.

6. A tourist ______________________ a policeman.

b) *Answer the questions, please. Make short answers.*

1. Are the kids wearing jeans?	________, ______________________.
2. Are the men carrying boxes?	________, ______________________.
3. Is the boy reading a comic?	________, ______________________.
4. Is the woman driving a taxi?	________, ______________________.
5. Are the two ladies running?	________, ______________________.
6. Is the tourist asking a question?	________, ______________________.

© Persen Verlag

*Exercise 2	Olivia's dream

The night after her great birthday party with lots of chips and cola Olivia has a bad dream.

She is standing in a clothes shop with her friend Joan, and she is trying on a lot of new clothes:
- A red pullover, but Joan is laughing: "Terrible!"
- Blue jeans, but Joan is telling her: "Too long!"
- A yellow skirt, but Joan is shouting: "Too short!"
- Black trousers, but Joan is shouting louder: "Too big!"
- A blue shirt, but Joan is screaming: "Too small!"

Olivia is getting warmer and warmer. Joan is shouting louder and louder ...

Her brother comes in.
"Hey, Olivia, why are you shouting? And it's hot in here. Open a window."

Read the story and put the sentences right.

<u>*Example:*</u>
Olivia is standing in a music shop.
No, she isn't. She is standing in a clothes shop.

1. She is trying new guitars.

__________, ____________________. ____.

2. Joan is crying.

__________, ____________________. ____.

3. Olivia is trying on red trousers.

__________, ____________________. ____.

4. Joan is whispering: "Too big!"

__________, ____________________. ____.

5. Olivia is getting colder and colder.

__________, ____________________. ____.

Manfred Bojes: Grundwissen englische Grammatik – 5./6. Klasse
© Persen Verlag

*Exercise 3	Making questions

Find the questions and the short answers.

Example:

Jenny – work at a kitchen table

Is Jenny working at a kitchen table?

No, she isn't. She is working at a computer.

1. Lucky and Jonathan – go for a walk?

   ____?

   No, ________________. They are going for a ride.

2. Larry – lie in bed?

   ____?

   No, ________________. He is lying in the sun.

3. you – have hamburgers from the snack bar?

   ____?

   No, ________________. We are having them from the tuck shop.

4. the Millers – ride their pony?

   ____?

   No, ________________. They are riding their motorbike.

5. you – make smoke signals?

   ____?

   No, ________________. I'm making a fire.

6. Sheila – sit at the doctor's?

   ____?

   No, ________________. She is sitting at the hairdresser's.

© Persen Verlag

Exercise 4 — A letter salad

There are six sentences in the salad. Write them down, please.

Awomanandamanarecleaningtheircartwogirlsareplayingintheroadis
tomgoingforawalkwithafriendnoheisn'theiscominghomefromschool
thesunisn'tshiningtodayandthepeoplearecarryingumbrellas

1. ____.
2. ____.
3. ____?
4. __________, __________________.
5. ____.
6. ____.

*Exercise 5 — Your turn

a) *Please write down what you are not doing at the moment.*

1. ____.
2. ____.
3. ____.
4. ____.

b) *Please write down what your brother, sister, mother, father is doing or what your friends are doing just now.*

1. ____.
2. ____.
3. ____.
4. ____.

© Persen Verlag

21. Mengenangaben

Wenn du im Englischen Mengenangaben bilden möchtest, verwendest du das Wort ***of***.

Beispiele:

a bar of chocolate	eine Tafel Schokolade
two boxes of apples	zwei Kisten Äpfel
four bottles of cola	vier Flaschen Cola
a glass of water	ein Glas Wasser
a pound of salt	ein Pfund Salz

Wenn du die Beispiele liest, fällt dir sofort auf, worin der Unterschied zum Deutschen besteht: In unserer Sprache fehlt das Wort ***of***.

Wenn du im Englischen „viel“ oder „viele“ ausdrücken willst, verwendest du ***a lot of***.

Beispiele:

I have got a lot of books in my room.
My cousin drinks a lot of milk.
We often make a lot of noise in the classroom.

In Fragen und Verneinungen dagegen benutzt du die Wörter ***much*** **(viel)** bei **nicht zählbaren Dingen** und ***many*** **(viele)** bei **zählbaren Dingen** und bei **Personen**.

Beispiele:

How many apples have you got?	Wie viele Äpfel hast du?
I haven't got many apples.	Ich habe nicht viele Äpfel.
How much time have we got?	Wie viel Zeit haben wir?
We haven't got much time.	Wir haben nicht viel Zeit.
How many pupils are there in your class?	Wie viele Schüler seid ihr in eurer Klasse?
Not many. Only eighteen.	Nicht viele. Nur achtzehn.

Manchmal findest du ***many*** auch in bejahten Aussagesätzen. Es bedeutet dann „viele verschiedene …“ oder „etliche …“

Beispiele:

Many people take the bus to go shopping in the city.
You can see many different kinds of big cats at the zoo.
Many pupils like Spanish but they can't learn it at our school.

Exercise 1 — What goes together?

A	glass bottle piece bag box packet bar bucket slice cup	of	water chocolate bread cake apples lemonade tape milk crisps chips cheese cornflakes

Put the pieces together, please.

1. ______________________
2. ______________________
3. ______________________
4. ______________________
5. ______________________
6. ______________________
7. ______________________
8. ______________________
9. ______________________
10. ______________________
11. ______________________
12. ______________________

Exercise 2 — Getting ready for shopping

Put in: *a lot of – much – many*

1. Mum, how ______________ tomatoes do we need for the salad?

   Well, we need ______________ tomatoes, ten or twelve.

2. And how ______________ bananas can I buy?

   You needn't buy so ______________ bananas. Two or three.

3. How ______________ sugar do you want? Not so ______________, one pound.

4. How ______________ milk do we need for the cake?

   We need ______________ milk. Buy four packets, please.

Manfred Bojes: Grundwissen englische Grammatik – 5./6. Klasse
© Persen Verlag

22. Die einfache Vergangenheit (*simple past*)

Wenn du etwas ausdrücken möchtest, das schon vorbei ist, bringst du die Verben, die dabei verwendet werden, in die Vergangenheitsform (*past form*). Das ist im Deutschen genauso wie im Englischen. Im Englischen wird es aber wesentlich einfacher gemacht:

An die meisten Verben hängst du nur *-ed* an, und fertig ist die Vergangenheitsform.
Das he/she/it -s entfällt sogar auch noch. Man nennt diese Verben **regelmäßige** Verben.

Beispiele:

Gegenwart (simple present)	Vergangenheit (simple past)
I look at my poster.	I looked at my poster.
We listen to our teacher.	We listened to our teacher.
She likes pets.	She liked pets.

Eine **Schwierigkeit** gibt es aber doch noch:

Bei einigen Verben funktioniert das Anhängen von *-ed* nicht; sie haben eine andere Vergangenheitsform. Man nennt diese Verben daher auch **unregelmäßige** Verben.

Beispiele:

Gegenwartsform	Vergangenheitsform
go	went
have/has	had
do	did
am/is (von „be")	was
are (von „be")	were
see	saw

Die Vergangenheitsformen solcher unregelmäßigen Verben kannst du am besten einzeln wie Vokabeln lernen.

© Persen Verlag

Willst du Fragen oder Verneinungen in die Vergangenheitsform setzen, so kannst du überall dort, wo *do/does* verwendet wird, diese Wörter einfach durch das Wort *did* ersetzen. Aus *don't* und *doesn't* wird dann *didn't*.

Beispiele:

Gegenwart (simple present)	Vergangenheit (simple past)
Do you like the oranges?	Did you like the oranges?
I don't eat oranges.	I didn't eat oranges.
Does she drink cola?	Did she drink cola?
No, she doesn't drink cola.	No, she didn't drink cola.
Where do they eat?	Where did they eat?
What does he eat?	What did he eat?

Fragen, die mit *did* beginnen, kannst du auch in einer Kurzform beantworten. Dazu benötigst du dann wieder *did* oder *didn't*.

Beispiele:

Did you like the oranges?	– Yes, I did.
Did she drink cola?	– No, she didn't.
Did you watch the film?	– Yes, we did.
Did the people in the film wear new clothes?	– No, they didn't.

Fragen und Verneinungen, die in der Gegenwart ohne *do/does* gebildet werden, werden auch ohne *did/didn't* in die Vergangenheit gesetzt.

Beispiele:

Gegenwart (simple present)	Vergangenheit (simple past)
I can't see the entrance.	I couldn't see the entrance.
He is not here.	He was not here.
We aren't in Wales.	We weren't in Wales.
Are you behind me?	Were you behind me?
Are you ill?	Were you ill?
Is she in Wales?	Was she in Wales?

Manfred Bojes: Grundwissen englische Grammatik – 5./6. Klasse
© Persen Verlag

Exercise 1 — Sheila's holidays

Put in the simple past forms of: *walk – be (3×) – stay – have – look – buy – go – see*

1. Sheila and her family ____________ at a bed and breakfast at the seaside.
2. They usually ____________ breakfast at nine.

3. Then they ____________ to the beach.
4. Her mother ____________ surfing, and her father ____________ after the baby.
5. The weather ____________ fine.

6. There ____________ no bad days.
7. Sheila's classmate Oliver ____________ on the beach, too.
8. She ____________ him when he ____________ some sweets at the little tuck shop.

Exercise 2 — Nora's present and past salad

Find the present and past forms and write them down, please.

Example: 1. difn – nofud
find – found

2. erid – dore
____________ – ____________

3. etirw – rotew
____________ – ____________

4. og – newt
____________ – ____________

5. espak – kespo
____________ – ____________

6. nigs – nags
____________ – ____________

7. nowk – newk
____________ – ____________

8. tea – aet
____________ – ____________

9. nur – nar
____________ – ____________

10. lafl – lefl
____________ – ____________

11. vige – vage
____________ – ____________

12. tup – tup
____________ – ____________

© Persen Verlag

*Exercise 3	Holiday acitivities

Put in the present or the past forms.

1. (*go*) The Prescotts always ___________ to the mountains, but last summer they ___________ to the seaside.
2. (*make*) Olly and Sam Prescott often ___________ things with their father. In their last holidays they ___________ a kite.
3. (*take*) Their baby brother Ronny often ___________ a teddy with him. This year he ___________ two.
4. (*run, fall*) When little Ronny ___________, he often ___________ down; in the last holidays he always ___________, but he never ___________ down.
5. (*drive*) Mrs Prescott usually ___________ the car, but this year Mr Prescott ___________ it.
6. (*do*) Mrs Prescott: "I often ___________ crossword puzzles in my holidays, but last summer I ___________ not do them at all".

*Exercise 4	Your turn

a) *Write down two things you did yesterday.*

1. ____.
2. ____.

b) *Write down two things your friends did yesterday.*

1. ____.
2. ____.

Manfred Bojes: Grundwissen englische Grammatik – 5./6. Klasse
© Persen Verlag

Exercise 5 — Did you have nice holidays?

Complete the sentences, please.

1. ___________ ________ have nice holidays? – No, we ____________.
2. ___________ ________ stay at a hotel? – Yes, we ____________.
3. ___________ ________ rain a lot? – Yes, ______ _________.
4. ________ your parents take you for long walks? – Yes, ______ _________.
5. ________ you like those walks? – No, I ______________.
6. ________ your baby sister tease you very often? – Yes, ___________. That's why I didn't like the holidays.

Exercise 6 — Sheila's weekend in Scotland

Read the answers and the questions first.

1. To Scotland.
2. At her aunt's house.
3. Yes, she did.
4. On Friday afternoon.
5. Yes, it rained all the time.
6. She went to Selkirk.
7. They all drove to Melrose Abbey.
8. On Sunday evening.

a) When did she arrive?
b) Did she go by bus?
c) What did she do on Saturday?
d) Where did Sheila go?
e) Where did she stay?
f) When did Sheila go home?
g) What did they all do on Sunday?
h) Did it rain?

a) *Now match the answers and the questions; put the right letters behind the numbers.*

1. ______ 2. ______ 3. ______ 4. ______ 5. ______ 6. ______ 7. ______ 8. ______

*b) *Can you ask Sheila three questions about her weekend?*

1. ____?

2. ____?

3. ____?

© Persen Verlag

Exercise 7	Tony's birthday party

Sam talked to his cousin Tony on the phone.
He had a lot of questions.

Complete the questions, please.

1. Wh________ ________ you have your last party?

   On the Friday after my birthday.

2. Wh________ ________ you have the party?

   At home in the hall.

3. ______________ all your friends come?

   Yes, they did.

4. Wh________ presents _________ they bring?

   They brought MP3s, books, a poster and a lot of chocolate.

5. ________ ________ you do after having tea?

   We listened to music and danced.

6. And then after that, _________ you play games?

   Yes, we played "Fancy Dress" with old clothes. It was a wild game.

7. Wh________ ________ your parents say about that?

   They didn't really like it. We shouted a lot.

8. H_______ long __________ your friends stay?

   They went home about nine p.m.

9. Wh________ ________ you go to bed?

   About half past ten because there was no school the next day.

10. H____________ ___________ hours _________ you sleep?

    I'm not sure. I think I slept until about ten a.m. because I was so tired.

Manfred Bojes: Grundwissen englische Grammatik – 5./6. Klasse
© Persen Verlag

23. Die Steigerung von Adjektiven

Du kannst Adjektive, mit denen du Personen oder Gegenstände beschreibst, steigern.

Es gibt im Englischen zwei Arten, Adjektive zu steigern.

1. Die Steigerung **durch Anhängen von *-er* und *-est***

   a) bei einsilbigen Adjektiven

   Beispiele:

   small – smaller – the smallest
   high – higher – the highest
   wet – wetter – the wettest
   big – bigger – the biggest
   old – older – the oldest
   nice – nicer – the nicest

   Die Beispiele zeigen (bei *big* und *wet*), dass sich der Endkonsonant verdoppelt, wenn davor ein kurzer Vokal steht. Ein stummes, also nicht ausgesprochenes -*e* (z. B. bei *nice*) fällt in beiden Steigerungsstufen auch beim Schreiben weg.

   b) bei zweisilbigen Adjektiven, die auf -*y* enden

   Beispiele:

   funny – funnier – the funniest
   heavy – heavier – the heaviest
   dirty – dirtier – the dirtiest
   angry – angrier – the angriest

   Die Beispiele zeigen, dass bei beiden Steigerungsstufen das -*y* zu -*i*- wird.

2. Die Steigerung mit ***more*** und ***the most.***
   Diese Steigerungsform benutzt man bei allen anderen Adjektiven mit zwei oder noch mehr Silben.

   Beispiele:

   famous – more famous – the most famous
   exciting – more exciting – the most exciting
   important – more important – the most important
   useful – more useful – the most useful
   modern – more modern – the most modern

© Persen Verlag

Es gibt zwei wichtige **Ausnahmen**. Das sind die englischen Wörter für „gut“ und „schlecht“:

good – better – the best **bad – worse – the worst**

Du kannst sie am besten wie Vokabeln lernen.

Wenn du die gesteigerten Adjektive in Vergleichssätzen anwenden willst, benutzt du die folgenden Muster:

a) **than = als**

Beispiele:
My grandma is older than my mum. My baby sister is younger than I.
French is more difficult than English.

b) **as ... as = so ... wie**

Beispiele:
New York is as big as London. Maths is as important as German.
Tim is as old as Anne.

c) **not as ... as = nicht so ... wie**

Beispiele:
New York is not as old as London. Cologne is not as big as New York.
A car is not as expensive as a plane.

Lerntipp:
Das Wort ***than*** (= als) in einem Satz mit einer Steigerungsform (*bigger than, more careful than, more terrible than, younger than*) darfst du nicht verwechseln mit ***then*** (= dann)!

Manfred Bojes: Grundwissen englische Grammatik – 5./6. Klasse
© Persen Verlag

Exercise 1 — Opposites

Connect the opposites, please.

the fastest	cheap
warmer than	luckier than
worse than	careful
the highest	difficult
boring	interesting
easy	the slowest
unhealthier than	pretty
the most useful	the dirtiest
expensive	full
shorter than	colder than
stupid	the lightest
careless	the lowest
the cleanest	healthier than
later than	clever
empty	the most useless
the heaviest	longer than
unluckier than	better than
ugly	earlier than

© Persen Verlag

Exercise 2	Can you compare the things?

a) *Complete the sentences, please.*

Use: *bigger than – the biggest*

1. The school is ________________ ________________ the house.
2. The skyscraper is ________________ ________________ the school.
3. The skyscraper _____ ____________________ ________ the house and the school.
4. The skyscraper _______ ______ ________________________.

*b) *Write down three sentences and compare these things:*

1. ***old***: London – New York – Rome

____.

____.

____.

2 ***expensive***: car – bike – plane

____.

____.

____.

Manfred Bojes: Grundwissen englische Grammatik – 5./6. Klasse
© Persen Verlag

Exercise 3	Good birthday presents

Compare the things and complete the sentences.

1. *cheap*

   A music DVD is ____________________ _______ a new bag for a notebook,

   but a poster is the ____________________.

2. *expensive*

   Tennis balls are _______ ______________ _______ table tennis balls,

   but a new basketball is _______ ____________ ________________.

3. *funny*

   A comic is ____________________ ______ an animal poster, but a comedy film

   is ______ ____________________.

4. *large*

   A map of Britain is __________________ ______ a city map, but a giant colour

   poster of the earth is ______ __________________.

5. *bad*

   A school history book is usually ________________ ______ a book about wildlife,

   but a Maths exercise book is ______ ______________ birthday present for Emma.

Exercise 4	Make comparisons.

Put in the missing forms of the adjectives, please.

1. stupid – ______________________ – ______________________
2. ______________________ – ______________________ – the most polite
3. ______________________ – hotter – ______________________
4. important – ______________________ – ______________________
5. ______________________ – ______________________ – the happiest
6. ______________________ – more terrible – ______________________

© Persen Verlag

Exercise 5	School gossip

Complete the sentences and use: *is as … as – isn't as … as*

1. *young*

   Mr Dorsey is a young teacher, he's 26. Mrs Tracy is 26, too.

   She ______________________________ Mr Dorsey.

2. *difficult*

   Of course History ______________________________ Maths.

3. *interesting*

   The music in the Music lessons ______________________________ pop music.

4. *nice*

   Mr Brown is nice and Mr Dorsey is nice, too.

   So Mr Brown ______________________________ Mr Dorsey.

*Exercise 6	Your friends and family

Compare your friends and/or your family.

You can use: *tall – old – young – small – nice – healthy – modern*

1. ____.
2. ____.
3. ____.
4. ____.
5. ____.
6. ____.

Manfred Bojes: Grundwissen englische Grammatik – 5./6. Klasse
© Persen Verlag

24. Bestätigungsfragen (*question tags*)

Im Deutschen benutzt du am Ende von Aussagen oft bestimmte Wörter, um von einem Gesprächspartner eine Zustimmung zu erhalten, z. B.
„Die Hose steht mir, **oder**?"
„Die Hose steht mir, **nicht wahr**?"
„Das Haus schaut gut aus, **gell**?"

Im Englischen gibt es solche Bestätigungsfragen (*question tags*) oder Frageanhängsel ebenfalls.

Das Verb des Satzes wird dabei erneut aufgegriffen und das Subjekt des Satzes wird zu einem Personalpronomen.

Wenn das Verb im Satz bejaht ist, wird es in der Bestätigungsfrage verneint; wenn es im Satz verneint ist, wird es bejaht.

<u>Beispiele:</u>

The new hotel is big, **isn't it**?
The drinks are for us, **aren't they**?
Paul can meet Sue at the station, **can't he**?
I'm not really ill, **am I**?
Your birthday isn't today, **is it**?
We aren't late, **are we**?
She is not listening, **is she**?
You're dreaming, **aren't you**?

Diese Beispielsätze enthalten alle ein Hilfsverb oder eine Form von „to be". Bei Sätzen ohne Hilfsverb (oder „to be") verwendest du in den Frageanhängseln eine Form von ***do***.

<u>Beispiele:</u>

We play table tennis, **don't we**?
Dad comes home in the evening, **doesn't he**?
You read detective stories, **don't you**?
You don't like meat, **do you**?
Olivia doesn't play tennis, **does she**?
Sam and Tony don't speak Spanish, **do they**?

Wie du an allen Beispielsätzen erkennen kannst, musst du die Bestätigungsfrage immer mit einem Komma von dem vorangehenden Aussagesatz trennen.

© Persen Verlag

Exercise 1	Question tags are easy, aren't they?

Find the correct question tags and put them in, please.

1. Your brother is twelve, ____________________? (is he / isn't he)
2. My pen is here on the table, ____________________? (isn't it / is it)
3. Tony and Sue are in Year 8, ____________________? (are they / aren't they)
4. My cat is nice, ____________________? (isn't it / is it)
5. We aren't in the right tuck shop, ____________________? (are we / aren't we)
6. I'm not looking silly, ____________________? (am I not / am I)
7. Mr Dorsey teaches Maths, ____________________? (does he / doesn't he)
8. Our teachers don't read comics, ____________________? (do they / don't they)

*Exercise 2	Are these question tags easy, too?

Find the question tags and put them in, please.

1. Our parents aren't angry, ______________________________?
2. Mr Green doesn't teach Music, ______________________________?
3. You're not watching him, ______________________________?
4. It's raining, ______________________________?
5. The boys like rugby, ______________________________?
6. Paula plays basketball, ______________________________?
7. I'm not late, ______________________________?
8. You can play the guitar, ______________________________?

© Persen Verlag

25. Das *present perfect*

Wenn du ausdrücken möchtest, dass sich etwas zwar in der Vergangenheit ereignete, aber Auswirkungen bis in die Gegenwart hat – und auch Ergebnisse, die in der Gegenwart noch erkennbar sind, – verwendest du das *present perfect.*

Die Bildung dieser Zeitform ist der des deutschen Perfekts sehr ähnlich.
Man braucht dazu lediglich:

have + **3. Form des Verbs (*past participle*).**
has (bei: *he/she/it*)

Bei den regelmäßigen Verben wird die 3. Form des Verbs genau wie bei der 2. Form durch Anhängen von *-ed* gebildet.

Beispiele:

Look, I have cleaned my room. It's tidy now.
Tony has opened the window. The air is getting better.
We have climbed the mountain. What a wonderful view!
The kids have learned the new words. They are getting good marks in the test.

Bei den unregelmäßigen Verben unterscheidet sich die 3. Form des Verbs von der 2. Form. Genau wie die zweiten Formen kannst du sie am besten wie Vokabeln lernen.

An den Beispielsätzen kann man auch gut sehen, dass die beiden Teile des *present perfect* in Aussagesätzen immer zusammenbleiben und nicht durch andere Satzteile wie Objekte getrennt werden können.

Es gibt aber eine **Ausnahme**:
Bestimmte Wörter, die ein Signal geben, dass man das *present perfect* verwenden muss, dürfen zwischen *have/has* und der dritten Form stehen. Man nennt sie auch **Signalwörter**. Die am häufigsten verwendeten Signalwörter sind: *just, already, ever, never.*

Beispiele:

She has just cleaned her room.
They have never been in Canada.
Have you ever seen a white elephant?
We have already met the Princess of Wales.

Ein weiteres häufiges Signalwort beim *present perfect* ist *(not) yet.*

© Persen Verlag

In Fragen wird *yet* meistens anstatt *already* verwendet.
In Verneinungen wird *not* (bzw. *-n't*) *yet* in der Bedeutung von „noch nicht" gebraucht.

Beispiele:

Have you phoned your grandma yet?
No, I haven't phoned her yet.
Has your penfriend's email arrived yet?
No, it hasn't arrived yet.
Sue, you haven't done your homework yet!

An den Beispielen siehst du schon: Die Bildung von Fragen und Verneinungen im *present perfect* ist fast wie im Deutschen und daher sehr leicht.
Bei den Antworten kann man sich – wenn man will – auch mit Kurzantworten begnügen.

Beispiele:

Have you just opened the door? Yes, I have.
Has Tina ever been to California? No, she hasn't.
Have the girls ridden their horses? Yes, they have.
Have we finished all our work yet? No, we haven't.

Lerntipp:
Das intensive Lernen der drei Formen der unregelmäßigen Verben ist sehr wichtig, weil sie später in weiteren Zeitformen immer wieder gebraucht werden. Sie werden am Ende jedes Schüler-Englischbuches alphabetisch aufgeführt und lassen sich dort am besten üben.

Manfred Bojes: Grundwissen englische Grammatik – 5./6. Klasse
© Persen Verlag

Exercise 1 | Joshua, Lucy and Bonzo

Write down the sentences in the right order.
If they are questions, answer them, please.

1. never / to London. / Joshua / been / has

   ____

2. he / visited / already / has / Manchester and Liverpool. / but

   ____

3. come back from / just / has / his older sister Lucy / a trip to Wales.

   ____

4. Lucy: I / the key to my suitcase. / lost / have

   "______________________________

   Where is it?"

5. Lucy: it, / you / Dad? / seen / have

   "______________________________"

   Dad: "No, ______________________________"

6. Joshua: have / it / perhaps / you / in Wales. / left

   "______________________________"

7. Lucy: hasn't / out of the room? / walked / just / Bonzo

   "______________________________"

8. Mum: "Yes, ______________________________."

9. Lucy: the key! / he / taken / has / then

   "______________________________

   Hey, Bonzo, come back! You're a bad dog!"

© Persen Verlag

Exercise 2 | What have they just done in Keswick?

a) *Look at the pictures and write six sentences.*
Use the present perfect and take these verbs, please:

write – leave – paint – eat – read – do

1. Jack ______________________ his homework.
2. Bonzo ______________________ his dog food.
3. The teachers ______________________ their school.
4. Mrs Green ______________________ the newspaper.
5. Tanya ______________________ a text message.
6. Mr and Mrs May ______________________ a door.

*b) *Complete the questions and make short answers, please.*

Use these verbs: *clean – watch – leave – play – write – help*

1. ________ Jack ____________ his mother? No, ____________________.
2. ________ Bonzo ____________ TV? No, ____________________.
3. ________ the teachers ____________ their school? Yes, ____________________.
4. ________ Mrs Green ____________ her house? No, ____________________.
5. ________ Tanya ____________ a text message? Yes, ____________________.
6. ________ Mr and Mrs May ____________ a game? No, ____________________.

Manfred Bojes: Grundwissen englische Grammatik – 5./6. Klasse
© Persen Verlag

Exercise 3	**Where are they?**

Complete the sentences with the correct form of the present perfect, please.

steal – drink – see – take – fall – break – drive

1. Where's the milk?

   The cat ________________________ it.

2. Where are my beach shoes?

   They ________________________ into the water.

3. Where's our car?

   Mum ________________________ it into the garage.

4. Where's my MP3?

   ________________________ someone ________________________ it?

5. Where's my bike?

   ________________________ Tom ________________________ it?

6. Where's my bottle of Coke?

   I'm sorry, I ________________________ it.

7. Where are my rabbits?

   Oh, I ________________________ them in the garden.

© Persen Verlag

Exercise 4	Why – Because

a) *Complete the answers with the correct form of the present perfect and use "just", please.*

> *Example:*
> Why is Bonzo so lazy? he – eat – a lot of dog food
> Because he has just eaten a lot of dog food.

1. Why are you shouting, Jason? my dog – run away

   Because ______________________________.

2. Why is the teacher angry? the kids – draw – his face on the board

   Because ______________________________.

3. Why is Shani the cat running away? she – see – Bonzo the dog

   Because ______________________________.

4. Why are Cynthia and Tim sad? their father – have – an accident

   Because ______________________________.

5. Why is Mr Rock so happy? he – win – one million pounds

   Because ______________________________.

*b) *Now find three "Because-sentences" with or without "just" yourself.*

1. Why is Olivia's purse empty?

   Because ______________________________.

2. Why are all the kids in the class tired?

   Because ______________________________.

3. Why are you so thirsty, Jack?

   Because ______________________________.

Manfred Bojes: Grundwissen englische Grammatik – 5./6. Klasse
© Persen Verlag

Exercise 5	**Five o'clock in the afternoon**

It is five o'clock. This is what a few people in Keswick have just done:

1. Mr Cloud has put off his hat.
2. Kevin has cleaned his room.
3. Jack and Ben have been at the cinema.
4. Mrs Cloud has bought a newspaper.
5. Mr Block has checked the oil in his car.
6. The Browns have done their shopping.
7. Shani the cat has jumped into her basket.
8. Cynthia and Tim have visited their father in hospital.
9. Tanya has listened to the five o'clock radio news.
10. The teachers have finished their meeting.

They all did it yesterday, too, so put the sentences into simple past, please.

Yesterday

1. Mr Cloud ______________________________.
2. Kevin ______________________________.
3. Jack and Ben ______________________________.
4. Mrs Cloud ______________________________.
5. Mr Block ______________________________.
6. The Browns ______________________________.
7. Shani the cat ______________________________.
8. Cynthia and Tim ______________________________.
9. Tanya ______________________________.
10. The teachers ______________________________.

© Persen Verlag

*Exercise 6	Six o'clock in the afternoon

Have they done it? Use the present perfect ***and*** *the simple past to complete the dialogues.*

1. **Tim and Tom:**

"Tom, __________ you (learn) __________ for the German test yet?"

"No, I ____________________________."

"And what did you do?"

"I (play) ____________________________ basketball."

---

2. **Mother and Sarah:**

"____________ you (send) ________________ the birthday card for Aunt Marty yet, Sarah?"

"No, I ____________________________."

"So what did you do this afternoon?"

"I (go) ____________________________ shopping with Olivia and (look) ____________________________ for a nice present in the city."

---

3. **Father and Olivia:**

"__________ you just (be) __________ in the city?"

"Yes, I ____________________________."

"But it's your turn to wash up today, isn't it?"

"I know, but I (not do) ____________________________ it because Sarah (have) ____________________________ to look for a birthday present for her aunt."

Manfred Bojes: Grundwissen englische Grammatik – 5./6. Klasse
© Persen Verlag

*Exercise 7	I like Alaska.

Put in simple past or present perfect.

1. Our cousin Phil (go) ______________________________

   to Alaska in his holidays last year.
2. We (never – be) ______________________________ there.
3. But Phil (show) ______________________________ us lots of nice photos.
4. Last week I (buy)______________________________ a map of Alaska.
5. I (already – look) ______________________________ at it many times.
6. Yesterday my dad (have) ______________________________ a close look at it, too.

*Exercise 8	Your turn

a) *Please write down four things you did last weekend.*

1. ____.
2. ____.
3. ____.
4. ____.

b) *Please write down four things you haven't done yet today.*

1. ____.
2. ____.
3. ____.
4. ____.

© Persen Verlag

26. Das Possessivpronomen

Du hast bereits die Possessivbegleiter
my – your – his – her – its – our – your – their kennengelernt.

Sie sagen etwas darüber aus, wem etwas gehört oder zu wem etwas gehört. Die Possessivbegleiter heißen so, weil sie ein Nomen begleiten.

Beispiele:

Here is my sister Jane, and this is our cousin Norman.
We like his new car because its colour is red.

Wenn du jedoch ein Nomen nicht wiederholen möchtest, kannst du es nicht durch einen solchen Possessivbegleiter ersetzen, sondern du musst jetzt ein Possessivpronomen verwenden.

Die Possessivpronomen im Englischen lauten:

mine – meiner, meine, meins
yours – deiner, deine, deins (Anrede: Ihrer, Ihre, Ihrs)
his – seiner, seine, seins
hers – ihrer, ihre, ihrs
ours – unser, unsere, unsers
yours – euer, eure, euers (Anrede: Ihrer, Ihre, Ihrs)
theirs – ihr, ihre, ihrs

Beispiele:

This is your book, and that is **mine**.
Pam is looking for her MP3; that one over there must be **hers**.
This is our car, and those two bikes are **ours**, too.
Look, they are using the teacher's colour markers, they have lost **theirs**.
Is this your English book? No, it's **yours**.

An den Beispielen kannst du sehen, dass sich die **Possessivpronomen nicht verändern**, egal ob das Nomen, das von Ihnen ersetzt wird, im Singular oder im Plural steht.

© Persen Verlag

Exercise 1	At school

Put in the correct words, please.

1. Don't drink that lemonade. It's (my/mine) _________ lemonade.
2. Whose skateboards are these? – They're (their/theirs) _________.
3. Is this your poster? – No, it's (your/yours) _________, Sue and Pat.
4. Whose raincoat is that? – It's (her/hers) _________ raincoat.
5. Please bring us back those comics. – They're (our/ours) _________.
6. Are these your chairs, Tim and Tom? – No, they're (your/yours) _________ chairs.
7. Look at this smartphone. It's (my/mine) _________.
8. Whose blue and white trainers are these? –

   They're (their/theirs) _________ trainers.
9. Is that Jane's locker over there? – Yes, it's (her/hers) _________.
10. Is that your pen on the desk, Pat? – No, it's (your/yours) _________, Mr Brown.

Exercise 2	What belongs together?

Put in the right words.

<u>*Example:*</u> I – my – mine

1. you – your – _______________
2. he – _______________ – _______________
3. _______________ – _______________ – hers
4. we – _______________ – _______________
5. _______________ – their – _______________

© Persen Verlag

*Exercise 3	In the classroom

Change the second sentence in number 1.–8. and use possessive pronouns, please.

<u>Example:</u>
Where is my English book? – This here isn't my English book.
This isn't mine.

1. Is that really your jacket? – It doesn't look like your jacket.

   It ____.

2. Ben has put his bag on the table. – This here isn't his bag.

   This ____.

3. Are these Lucy's and Joshua's exercise books? – Oh yes, they lost their exercise books a few minutes ago.

   Oh yes, ____.

4. Are those Linda's sweets under the bag? – No, they're my sweets.

   No, ____.

5. Is this your blue pencil? – No, it's your pencil.

   No, ____.

6. Is that Sarah's new smartphone on the table ? – Yes, that's her smartphone.

   Yes, ____.

7. Whose sandwich is this? – It's my sandwich.

   It's ____.

8. Hey girls, are these your caps? – Yes, they're our caps.

   Yes, ____.

© Persen Verlag

27. Adverbien der Art und Weise

Mit Adverbien kannst du ausdrücken, **wie** jemand etwas macht oder **wie** etwas geschieht. Man kann sagen, sie geben eine Antwort auf die Frage: **How?**

Das Adverb hat seinen Namen deshalb, weil es sich fast immer auf ein Verb bezieht. Das Adjektiv, mit dem es eng verwandt ist, bezieht sich dagegen auf ein Nomen oder Pronomen.

Während im Deutschen Adjektiv und Adverb die gleiche Form haben (**Er** ist **schnell**. Er **geht schnell**), verändert sich im Englischen die Form des Adjektivs, wenn es zum Adverb wird.

Die meisten Adverbien werden so gebildet:

Adjektiv + *-ly*

Beispiele:

nice – nicely loud – loudly slow – slowly quiet – quietly
Olivia is a nice singer. She sings nicely. Ben is slow. He runs slowly.

Ein *-le* am Ende eines Adjektivs wird beim Adverb zu *-ly*.

Beispiele:

terrible – terribly comfortable – comfortably
The storm is terrible. It is blowing terribly.

Ein *-y* am Ende eines Adjektivs wird beim Adverb zu *-i-*.

Beispiele:

happy – happily angry – angrily busy – busily easy – easily
The kids are happy. They are laughing happily. Mrs Croft is angry.
She is looking angrily.

Adjektive, die auf *-ic* enden, werden durch *-ally* ergänzt.

Beispiele:

fantastic – fantastically basic – basically
This song is fantastic. It sounds fantastically.

Es gibt drei wichtige Ausnahmen:
Das Adverb von ***good*** heißt ***well***. Das Adverb von ***fast*** heißt ***fast***.
Das Adverb von **hard** heißt **hard**.

© Persen Verlag

Exercise 1	How?

Find the right adverbs and write them in the gaps, please.

fast – well – crazily – busily – happily – quietly – carefully –
hard – fantastically – terribly

1. Peggy is happy. She is singing ________________.
2. She is a good singer. She can sing ________________.
3. A taxi driver is careful. He drives ________________.
4. My friend Tom is a fantastic tennis player. He plays ________________.
5. Pat's handwriting is terrible. She writes ________________.
6. Pam is always fast when she writes. She writes too ________________.
7. Sue's German homework is hard. She works ________________ to answer the questions.
8. Mrs Loft is busy. She ________________ phones her friends every day.
9. Ben is a quiet boy. He always listens ________________ when his friends talk.
10. Ricky Riverside is a crazy guitar player. He always plays his guitar ________________.

© Persen Verlag

Exercise 2	Tom the tennis champion

Change the adjectives into adverbs and write the sentences down.

1. Tom can (easy) play tennis for hours.

   ____.

2. He usually plans his matches (careful).

   ____.

3. Every day he practises (busy) to get better.

   ____.

4. But of course he can already play very (good).

   ____.

5. After a match he (thirsty) drinks two bottles of water.

   ____.

*Exercise 3	More Hobbies

Adverb or adjective? -ly or not? Use the words in the box.

hungry – beautiful – quiet – cheap – loud – happy

1. Steve is a drummer. He likes to play his drums l______________.
2. Angie is h______________ when she can q______________ sit in her room and read an interesting book.
3. Mr McBeef's hobby is eating, because he is always h______________.
4. Emma and Tina like dancing. They really dance b______________.
5. Tim's hobby is shopping. He often looks for c______________ clothes.

© Persen Verlag

28. Das *will-future*

Mit dem *will-future* kannst du etwas voraussagen, z. B.in Form einer Wettervorhersage oder eines Horoskops.

Beispiele:

Tomorrow it will be cold in London.

Du kannst das *will-future* auch verwenden, wenn du dich spontan für etwas entscheidest.

Beispiele:

You're ill? I will come and do the shopping for you.

Du gebrauchst das *will-future* auch, um zukünftige Ereignisse oder Tatsachen auszudrücken, auf die du keinen Einfluss hast.

Beispiele:

I will be twenty in six years.

Für die Bildung des *will-future* gibt es eine einfache Formel:

will **+ Grundform des Verbs (Infinitiv)**

Beispiele:

Shani will look older in 20 years.
The lessons wil start in a few minutes.

Beim Sprechen benutzt du die Kurzform mit ***'ll*** in bejahten und ***won't*** *(= will not)* in verneinten Aussagen.

Beispiele:

He's late. I'm sure he'll miss the bus.
He won't be at school in time.

Du kannst dir als Hilfe auch einige **Signalwörter** merken, die dir anzeigen, dass du das *will-future* verwenden musst:

perhaps, probably, to be sure, to hope, to think

Beispiele:

I think I'll be home at one o'clock.
We'll probably have lunch then.
Perhaps Dad won't be in time then.

Manfred Bojes: Grundwissen englische Grammatik – 5./6. Klasse
© Persen Verlag

Exercise 1	Before the weekend

Put in "will" or "won't".

1. The weatherman says it ______________ be nice tomorrow and there ______________ be any clouds. So we needn't take umbrellas when we go to the seaside.
2. On Sunday Steve and Angie ______________ be at Don's birthday party, but Tim ______________ be there; he is in hospital for a few days.
3. The sports shop ______________ be open on Sunday, so they ______________ buy Don a new tennis racket on Saturday.
4. They ______________ stay too long at the party because there ______________ be school on Monday morning, of course.
5. The next holidays ______________ start in two weeks. Until then they are sure they ______________ have a hard time with a lot of tests.
6. Steve is afraid. Perhaps he ______________ pass the Maths test.
7. But he hopes he ______________ have time to learn with his friends a few days before the test.
8. They all ______________ be happy if they can help him.
9. And perhaps the exercises in the test ______________ be too difficult at last.
10. So there ______________ be another party after an easy Maths test.

© Persen Verlag

***Exercise 2**	**We like History.**

It's the last lesson before the weekend starts. Mr Hicks, the History teacher, tries to teach the kids, but they are a bit tired of him.

Use "will" or "won't" and the following verbs to fill the gaps:

be (3×) – come – need – dream – copy – do

We ________ ________ lucky when it's over at last.

I hope the weekend ________ ________ as boring as Mr Hicks.

I'm hungry, I ________ ________ something to eat after the lesson.

I think Mr Hicks ________ ________ to school next Monday. He really looks ill.

Oh no, I ________ ________ my History homework. I ________ ________ it from Jane.

I hope I ________ ________ of History when I'm in bed tonight. That would be terrible!

Oh good, the lesson ________ ________ over in two minutes.

Manfred Bojes: Grundwissen englische Grammatik – 5./6. Klasse
© Persen Verlag

*Exercise 3	How can they help?

Write down how the people can help. Complete the sentences.
Use the will-future, please.

<u>Example:</u> 1. *show how*
Steve:
I'm not good at Maths. Can you help me with this exercise?
Angie and Don:
Of course, <u>we'll show you how</u> it works.

2. *look after*
Mum:
I'll have to go shopping in a minute. Can you play with your baby sister for an hour?
Steve:
No problem, ____ her.

3. *buy a new one*
Steve:
Oh, and, Mum, my exercise book is full. Can you bring a new one?
Mum:
Don't worry, ____ for you.

4. *help to look for*
Dad:
I can't find my glasses.
Mum:
Just a moment, ____ them.

5. *show the way*
Angie:
I want to go to the new cinema, but I don't know where it is.
Don:
No problem, ____.

6. *make some tea*
Grandma:
I'm not feeling too well. I'd really like a hot cup of tea.
Mrs. Loft:
Just a moment, ______________________________ for you, of course.

© Persen Verlag

Exercise 4	Good weather or bad weather?

Complete the sentences. Use "will" and "won't".

Example: *wear T-shirts*
The weather will be nice tomorrow, so the kids will wear T-shirts.

1. *take a hot shower*

   It ______ be cold and snowy, so Tim ________________ on Monday morning.

2. *have a garden party*

   Micky's birthday ______ be in December as every year, so he

   ________________________________.

3. *take umbrellas*

   It _____ rain a lot all evening long, so the people ______________ this evening.

4. *wear caps*

   Next week it ______ be cold, so the people ________________.

*Exercise 5	Micky's fortune telling

Please complete what the fortune teller says.

In ten years you ______ ________ a good job, but you ______ ________ a girlfriend, sorry. You ______ ________ in Germany, so you ______ visit your parents every weekend; but they ______ ________ too sad because you ______ always ______ nice presents for them. You ______ ________ in Germany for about two years, and then you ______ ________ home to Britain again.

Manfred Bojes: Grundwissen englische Grammatik – 5./6. Klasse
© Persen Verlag

29. Bedingungssätze (*if*-Sätze)

Bedingungssätze sind Sätze, die immer aus zwei Teilen bestehen:
aus einem ***if*-Satz** und einem **Hauptsatz.**

Im *if*-Satz wird eine Bedingung genannt, und im Hauptsatz wird ausgedrückt, was geschieht, wenn die Bedingung erfüllt wird.

Dabei steht der ***if*-Satz im *simple present*** und der **Hauptsatz im *will-future*.**

Das Wort ***if*** hat hier die Bedeutung: **falls, wenn**.

Es kann zuerst der *if*-Satz oder der Hauptsatz stehen.

Beispiele:

If the weather is nice this evening, we'll go for a walk.
If Peter and Mary come, we'll play games together.
You will not get good marks if you forget to do your homeworks.
You won't get good marks if you never learn the new words.
If I go shopping, I'll buy new jeans.
If we eat the cake today, there won't be any cake for tomorrow.

Wenn du sprichst oder etwas aufschreibst, das mündlich geäußert wurde, kannst du beim *will-future* wie gewohnt die Kurzform ***'ll*** statt ***will*** und ***won't*** statt ***will not*** verwenden.

© Persen Verlag

Exercise 1 | Timmy and Carla alone at home

The Cools are going out for a visit. This is what they tell their kids.

Match the two parts of the sentences and write them down.

1. If you send us a text message, …	… the mice will come in.
2. If you get any serious problems, …	… we won't wake you up.
3. If you want a TV magazine, …	… she'll want to know where we are.
4. If you need more tea, …	… the neighbours will help you.
5. If you want fresh bread, …	… we'll answer it.
6. If Grandma phones, …	… we'll tell you.
7. If you don't close the back door in the evening, …	… they will sell you some at the Bakers' after five p.m.
8. If it rains, …	… you will find it under the TV.
9. If we don't come home before nine p.m., …	… you'll have to go to the supermarket.
10. If you sleep when we arrive, …	… you'll have to take an umbrella when you go out.

1. ____.
2. ____.
3. ____.
4. ____.
5. ____.
6. ____.
7. ____.
8. ____.
9. ____.
10. ____.

© Persen Verlag

*Exercise 2	Mrs Cool is nervous.

Mr and Mrs Cool are going on a flight to Ireland.
Mrs Cool is very nervous; she thinks they'll miss
their flight.

a) This is what she says:
1. If we (not hurry), we (miss) our flight.
2. We (miss) the flight, too, if the shuttle bus (be) late.
3. If you (not be) dressed in a minute, I (fly) alone.
4. If you (not come) with me, I (feel) sorry for you.

Now write the sentences and use the correct verb forms.

1. ____.
2. ____.
3. ____.
4. ____.

b) But Mr Cool keeps cool. He thinks:
1. I (go) crazy if she (not stop) shouting.
2. If I (not hurry), she (not leave) without me.
3. We (take) a taxi if the bus (be) late.
4. If I (stay) here, I (not feel) sorry.

Write the sentences and use the correct verb forms.

1. ____.
2. ____.
3. ____.
4. ____.

© Persen Verlag

Exercise 3	The Cools in Ireland

Write the complete sentences down and use the right verb forms.

1. If the weather (be) bad, the Cools' plane (not land) in Dublin.

____.

2. If they (can land) in Dublin, they (take) a taxi to their hotel.

____.

3. They (ask) the receptionist for a nice restaurant if they (go out).

____.

4. They (walk) into the city if it (not rain).

____.

*Exercise 4	Mediating

At the reception desk in the hotel Mr Cool helps an old German lady. She cannot speak English very well. But Mr Cool can speak German. He tells the receptionist what the German lady says.

„Wenn das Abendessen gut ist, komme ich später ins Hotelrestaurant. Ist die Hoteltür noch offen, falls ich nach 22 Uhr zurückkommen sollte? Ich werde noch eine Decke brauchen, falls es kalt im Zimmer ist. Wenn das Wetter schlecht ist, reise ich morgen ab."

Mr Cool:

"She says she ____

______________________________. She asks whether the door ________ still

________ open if ________ after 10 p.m. And she says she ________________

another blanket if ______________________________ too cold. And if the weather

______________________________ tomorrow".

____

Manfred Bojes: Grundwissen englische Grammatik – 5./6. Klasse
© Persen Verlag

Abbildungsnachweis

Seite 3: Netzwerk © rubysoho – Fotolia.com

Seite 14: „Twitter-Vogel“ URL:
http://commons.wikimedia.org/wiki/File:Twitschervogel01_derived_from_twitter-t.svg CC-BY-SA-3.0//Original uploader was User: GageSkidmore, modified by User: Cpro;
Laptop © Fatmann73 – Fotolia.com

Seite 18: Männchen mit Fragezeichen © AirOne – Fotolia.com

Seite 22: Männchen mit Fragezeichen © AirOne – Fotolia.com

Seite 26: MP3-Player © pizuttipics – Fotolia.com

Seite 48: diverse Verbotsschilder © vektorisiert – Fotolia.com

Seite 55: Müslischale mit Obst © HLPhoto – Fotolia.com

Seite 56: Männchen mit Fragezeichen © AirOne – Fotolia.com

Seite 57: Sänger © Designer_Andrea – Fotolia.com; Tischtennisschläger © milosluz – Fotolia.com; Tänzer © hibrida 13 – Fotolia.com; Tennisschläger © Dark Vecorangel – Fotolia.com; Portion Pommes © ExQuisine – Fotolia.com; Basketball © Marcito – Fotolia.com

Seite 62: Schild © sonya etchison – Fotolia.com

Seite 86: Kolosseum © fabiomax.com – Fotolia.com; New York © D.aniel – Fotolia.com

Seite 93: Hund © Finetti – Fotolia.com

Seite 95: MP3-Player © pizuttipics – Fotolia.com

Seite 97: Uhr © Ingrid Hecht

Seite 104: Piktogramm © Tonis Pan – Fotolia.com

Seite 109: Help-Button © vege – Fotolia.com

Fit in Englisch mit den Bergedorfern!

Claudine Steyer

Lernzielkontrollen Englisch

Tests in zwei Differenzierungsstufen

Zur gezielten Vorbereitung auf Klassenarbeiten und schriftliche Tests müssen Sie in der Sekundarstufe viel Zeit und Mühe investieren, um individuell passgenaue Übungsaufgaben zu konzipieren. Die Reihe „Lernzielkontrollen" bringt hier Unterstützung. Zu allen Themen der jeweiligen Fächer in den Klassen 5–10 der Haupt- und Realschulen bieten die Bücher strukturiertes Material zur Überprüfung des Leistungsstandes, zur Ermittlung des individuellen Förderbedarfs sowie zur Übung und Wiederholung. Aufgaben mit steigendem Schwierigkeitsgrad, Übungen auf zwei Niveaustufen und beigefügte Lösungsseiten helfen, den Leistungsstand jedes einzelnen Schülers einfach und sicher zu ermitteln.

So überprüfen Sie einfach und effektiv die Leistungsstände Ihrer Schüler!

Buch, 136 Seiten, DIN A4
5. bis 10. Klasse
Best.-Nr. 3373

Brigitte Penzenstadler

Learning English All Year Round

Attraktive Kopiervorlagen für das ganze Jahr

Abwechslungsreiche Arbeitsblätter, Rätsel und Spiele für jede Jahreszeit – was brauchen Sie mehr? Mit den Kopiervorlagen erweitern und festigen Sie durch spielerische Übungen den Wortschatz, trainieren grammatische Strukturen und schulen das Textverständnis. Toller Nebeneffekt: Auch das Verfassen eigener Texte im Sinne des Creative Writing wird angeregt. Und: Lösungsseiten bieten die Möglichkeit der Selbstkontrolle!

Das Rundum-Programm für Ihre Schülerinnen und Schüler: Vom Wortschatztraining zum Creative Writing!

Buch, 119 Seiten, DIN A4
5. bis 10. Klasse
Best.-Nr. 3795

Manfred Bojes

Grundwissen englische Grammatik 7./8. Klasse

Materialien in 2 Differenzierungsstufen

Sie sind auf der Suche nach Übungsmaterial für die grammatischen Themen des Englischunterrichts in der 7. und 8. Klasse? Hier werden Sie garantiert fündig. Zur Einführung wiederholt der Band die wichtigsten grammatischen Inhalte der Klassen 5 und 6, da diese für den weiteren Englischunterricht von grundlegender Bedeutung sind. So gleichen Sie die heterogenen Leistungsstände Ihrer Schüler, die häufig auch noch unsicher im Anwenden der neuen Sprache sind, an. Die Übungsaufgaben zu den grammatischen Themen der Klassen 7 und 8 sind in Situationen aus dem Alltag eingebettet. So erleben Ihre Schüler, dass Grammatik kein Selbstzweck ist, sondern eine wichtige kommunikative Funktion erfüllt. Die Aufgaben liegen in zwei Differenzierungsstufen vor. Jeder grammatische Inhalt wird kurz, übersichtlich und mit anschaulichen Beispielen eingeführt, sodass Ihre Schüler selbstständig mit den Übungsaufgaben arbeiten können. Auf der beiliegenden CD erhalten Sie die Lösungen zu allen Aufgaben.

Mit schülerorientierten Übungen die englische Grammatik systematisch erarbeiten!

Buch, 88 Seiten, DIN A4, inkl. CD
7. und 8. Klasse
Best.-Nr. 3032

Frauke Wietzke

A Reader's Diary

Strukturierte Vorlagen zur Erschließung englischer Texte

Englische Lektüre leicht gemacht! Die Mappe bietet eine Blanko-Version für ein Lesetagebuch, mit dem die Schüler selbstständig englische Texte lesen und bearbeiten können. Jede Menge „Blanko-Seiten" mit Fragestellungen und Arbeitsanweisungen, die den Leseprozess steuern und gestalten und die auf jede Lektüre übertragbar sind, erleichtern das Bearbeiten der Textvorlagen. Die Schüler setzen sich mithilfe der Kopiervorlagen intensiv mit dem Inhalt ihrer jeweiligen Lektüre auseinander, entwickeln (angeleitete) Lesestrategien und Sprachbewusstheit ebenso wie eigene Standpunkte zu dem jeweiligen Thema. Das motiviert, sich noch eingehender mit der Fremdsprache zu beschäftigen.

Das Lesetagebuch – jetzt auch für den Englischunterricht!

Mappe mit Kopiervorlagen, 43 Seiten, DIN A4
7. bis 10. Klasse
Best.-Nr. 2174

Unser Bestellservice:

Das komplette Verlagsprogramm finden Sie in unserem Online-Shop unter

www.persen.de

Bei Fragen hilft Ihnen unser Kundenservice gerne weiter.

Deutschland: ✆ 0 40/32 50 83-040 · Schweiz: ✆ 052/366 53 54 · Österreich: ✆ 0 72 30/2 00 11